Project Editor
Sarah Ann Schmidt

Consultant
Connie Spencer Ackerman
Consultant, Educational Services
Ohio Department of Education

Field-Test Coordinator
Charles Nystrom
College of Lake County
Waukegon, IL

CONTEMPORARY BOOKS

CHICAGO · NEW YORK

Library of Congress Cataloging-in-Publication Data

Echaore-Yoon, Susan, 1953–
    Reader's choice insights / Susan Echaore-Yoon.
        p.   cm.
        ISBN 0-8092-4427-6
    1. English language—Textbooks for foreign speakers.   I. Title.
PE1128.E27   1989
428.6'4—dc19

89-22125
CIP

Photo Credits
Page 1: © Lionel J.M. Delevingue/Stock Boston. Page 9: © Michael Hayman/TSW-Click/Chicago, Ltd. Page 17: © C. C. Cain Photography. Page 25: © Olof Kallstrom/Jeroboam. Page 28: © AP/Wide World Photos. Page 33: Courtesy of the Chicago Public Library. Page 41: © Hank Lebo/Jeroboam. Page 44: The Bettmann Archive. Page 49: Courtesy of the Milwaukee County Zoo. Page 57: © Stu Rosner/Stock Boston. Page 60: © Hazel Hankin/Stock Boston. Page 65: © Silver Image. Page 68: © Peter Menzel/Stock Boston. Page 73: © Frank Siteman. Page 81: AP/Wide World Photos. Page 84: AP/Wide World Photos. Page 89: © Emilio Mercado/Jeroboam.

Cover photo © C. C. Cain Photography

This book is an educational textbook. Names, characters, organizations, places, and incidents on pages 1, 9, 17, 25, 33, 41, 57, 65, 80, and 89 are used solely to illustrate the lessons contained herein and should not be considered real or factual. The persons portrayed in photographs on pages 1, 9, 17, 25, 33, 41, 57, 60, 65, 68, 80, and 89 are models. Their actions, motivations, and dialogue are entirely fictional. Any resemblance to actual persons, living or dead, and actual events, locales, or organizations is entirely coincidental.

Copyright © 1989 by Contemporary Books, Inc.
All rights reserved

No part of this publication may be reproduced, stored in a retrieval system, or transmitted in any form or by any means, without the prior written permission of the publisher.

Published by Contemporary Books, Inc.
180 North Michigan Avenue, Chicago, Illinois 60601
Manufactured in the United States of America
International Standard Book Number: 0-8092-4427-6

Published simultaneously in Canada by
Beaverbooks, Ltd.
195 Allstate Parkway
Valleywood Business Park
Markham, Ontario L3R 4T8
Canada

Editorial Director
Caren Van Slyke

Editorial
Kathy Osmus
Sarah Conroy
Craig Bolt
Mark Boone
Mary Banas
Robin O'Connor
Leah Mayes

Editorial/Production Manager
Patricia Reid

Cover Design
Lois Koehler

Illustrator
Guy Wolek

Photo Researcher
Julie Laffin

Art & Production
Andrea Haracz
Jan Geist
Princess Louise El

Typography
Terrence Alan Stone

Contents

Introduction v

PEOPLE

FAMILY STRUCTURES

The Invitation 1

The Five Ws ■ What Kind of Family? ■ Vocabulary ■
It's a Syllable! ■ A Family Tree

PARENTING STYLES

Single-Parent Dad 9

Details in the Newspaper ■ A Parent's Life ■ Vocabulary ■
Compound Words ■ Keeping Dates Straight

MARRIAGE TRENDS

Married or Single? 17

Please Restate That! ■ Graph It! ■ Vocabulary ■
End It! ■ Crossword Puzzle

ISSUES

REGISTERING TO VOTE

Does One Vote Make a Difference? 25

Summarizing ■ Signing Up ■ Vocabulary ■
More Endings ■ Fill It Out

THE BILL OF RIGHTS

My Right to Read 33

Finding a Main Idea ■ What's in the Bill? ■ Vocabulary ■
Begin It! ■ Using the Library

A NATION OF IMMIGRANTS

Crossing the Border 41

Finding Unstated Main Ideas ■ When and Why? ■ Vocabulary ■
Prefix + Word + Suffix ■ Conduct an Interview

WORK

CAREER CHOICES

Help Wanted............49

Predicting Words ■ What Do You Do? ■ Vocabulary ■
Short and Long ■ Career and Job Research

STARTING A JOB HUNT

Waiting............57

Infer It ■ Planning the Hunt ■ Vocabulary ■
Break It Up: VC/CV Rule ■ Getting Ready!

THE JOB INTERVIEW

Making It Work............65

More on Inferring ■ You Be the Job Counselor ■ Vocabulary ■
Break It Up: V/CV Rule ■ Getting It Right!

SCIENCE

THE FOUR FOOD GROUPS

Are You What You Eat?............73

Compare and Contrast ■ Serve It Up ■ Vocabulary ■
Break It Up: VC/V Rule ■ Be a Label Reader

THE FACTS ABOUT AIDS

The Battle Against AIDS............81

Cause and Effect ■ Just the Facts ■ Vocabulary ■
Break It Up: VC/CV, V/CV, and VC/V Rules ■ What's the Hypothesis?

SMOKING AND THE RESPIRATORY SYSTEM

"No Smoking!"............89

Sequencing ■ Full of Smoke ■ Vocabulary ■
Syllabication Rules Review ■ Keeping a Journal

Answer Key............97

Introduction

Welcome to *Insights*, the first book in Contemporary's *Reader's Choice* series. *Insights* explores personal issues that are important to everyday life—being part of a family, registering to vote, getting ready for a job interview. This book gives you the information you need in today's world.

Insights will also help you understand and think about what you read. You'll learn tips for remembering what you read and ways to figure out the meaning of new words.

Each lesson contains

- reading for pleasure
- skill instruction
- reading-skill practice
- background reading
- critical-thinking questions
- new vocabulary
- word skills
- an extra activity

The books in Contemporary's *Reader's Choice* series are a bridge to reading whatever you want to read—newspapers, magazines, books, or information at work.

We hope you enjoy the lessons and pictures in *Insights* and wish you luck with your studies.

*The Editors
Contemporary Books*

PEOPLE

The Invitation

Carmen Ruiz sat at her kitchen table. She fanned herself with the wedding invitation in her right hand. The Florida heat was bad this morning. It would only get hotter. Carmen gave her two-month-old son a bottle and read the wedding invitation again.

Her cousin Tony was getting married next Sunday in Manatí, Puerto Rico. Carmen was born in Manatí and grew up there. All of her relatives still lived there. They would all be at the wedding. Only Carmen, her husband, and their baby would be missing. Roberto, her husband, said they did not have enough money yet to go back home.

Carmen's family owned a farm near Manatí. They grew sugar cane on more than sixty acres of land. Carmen could remember helping her father and uncles in the fields. Even now, as she looked out her kitchen window, Carmen could almost see the thick stems and feel the rich sap of the sugar cane.

Ten months ago, Roberto told Carmen that they were going to leave Puerto Rico. "Listen to me," he said. "We will do better for ourselves in Miami. I am tired of farming, and in Miami I can find work in a business."

Even though Carmen had not wanted to leave her family behind, she knew that Roberto was happier in Florida. He seemed content. He did not want to fight with her anymore. He had pride in his work, and his job at the store was going very well.

Carmen thought of her parents and grandparents, her brothers, and her many aunts, uncles, and cousins. She pictured them at Tony's wedding, dancing and laughing. Carmen looked at the invitation one more time, then put it in a drawer where she could not see it. ■

Often, families move together from Puerto Rico to the United States.

SKILL BUILD

The Five Ws

WHO WHAT WHEN WHERE

Tony will be married Sunday in Manatí, Puerto Rico,

WHY

because he is in love.

The sentence above gives some important facts about the story you just read. It tells *who* will do *what*, and *when*, *where*, and *why* it will take place.

Each time you read something new, ask yourself these **five W questions**: *who*, *what*, *when*, *where*, and *why*. They will help you understand the important details in any story.

See how the five Ws can help you pick out other important details in the story you just read on page 1.

1. *Who* is the story about? _____

2. *What* is she doing? _____

3. *Where* does she live? _____

4. *When* did she leave Puerto Rico? _____

5. *Why* did she leave Puerto Rico? _____
_____

Your answers should be similar to these:

1. The story is about Carmen Ruiz.
2. Carmen is reading an invitation and thinking about her family.
3. She lives in Miami, Florida.
4. She and Roberto left Puerto Rico ten months ago.
5. Roberto wanted to find new work.

▼ POINT TO REMEMBER

Remember to ask yourself the five W questions—*who*, *what*, *when*, *where*, and *why*. They will help you find the important details in anything you read.

FIVE Ws PRACTICE

When you read an invitation to a party, what do you look for? Most likely, you check to see who or what the party is for and when and where to go.

Invitations give you quick, easy-to-find answers to the five W questions. They tell you *who*, *what*, *when*, *where*, and *why*.

Directions: Below are three invitations. Read them, then answer the questions that follow.

1. Please be our guest at a baby shower for Martha and Ed Baker.
   DATE AND TIME: Sunday, May 10, 4-6 P.M.
   PLACE: 218 Lake Street.

   a. *Who* is the party for? _____
   b. *What* kind of party is it? _____
   c. *When* will it take place? _____
   d. *Where* will it be held? _____
   e. *Why* will it take place? _____

2. Please help Kathy Allen and Charles Ferguson celebrate their first day of marriage. A reception will be held in Golden Gate Park on Saturday, September 21, 1-5 P.M.

   a. *Who* is the party for? _____
   b. *What* kind of party is it? _____
   c. *When* will it take place? _____
   d. *Where* will it be held? _____
   e. *Why* will it take place? _____

3. The Navarro children request your presence at a dinner honoring the 50th wedding anniversary of their parents, Marlene and Al Navarro.
   June 15, 1987, 12 P.M., Fort Ord Officers Club

   a. *Who* is the party for? _____
   b. *What* kind of party is it? _____
   c. *When* will it take place? _____
   d. *Where* will it be held? _____
   e. *Why* will it take place? _____

ONE MORE STEP

Directions: Imagine you are planning a party. Use the five Ws below to plan the party the way you would like.

Who is the party for?
_____
_____
_____

What kind of party is it?
_____
_____
_____

When will it take place?
_____
_____
_____

Where will it be held?
_____
_____
_____

Why will it take place?
_____
_____
_____

On a separate piece of paper, design an invitation for this party.

Family Structures

In the story you just read, where does Carmen's family live? If you think of two answers, you're right! Carmen, her husband, and their baby live in Miami. This is Carmen's **nuclear family**. The rest of Carmen's family live on a farm in Puerto Rico. This is Carmen's **extended family**. Both of these are family **structures**.

Like Carmen Ruiz, you are part of a nuclear family. Here, the word *nuclear* means center, or core, or heart. A nuclear

A nuclear family

family includes just parents and their children.

Like Carmen, you are also part of an extended family. Your extended family includes your nuclear family and all your other **relatives**.

Sometimes, the members of an extended family all live near one another. Grandparents, parents, and children may live in the same house. Aunts, uncles, and cousins live nearby.

Often, though, relatives live far away from each other. Your family may live in Los Angeles, while your grandparents live in Chicago and your cousins in New York. Do you know when American families started to spread out and live far from one another? Why did this happen?

Until the early 1900s, most extended families lived together in the same town. In many cases, the members of an extended family worked together to support the family farm or business. In the 1920s, though, two factors began to change American **society**.

An extended family

First, better **transportation** gave people more freedom. People could travel more often as well as farther because they had more cars and better roads.

Growing **industry** also changed American society. Shops and factories in every city needed workers. Many new jobs opened up, and people began moving to cities to fill those jobs.

Today, as in the 1920s, young adults often leave their hometowns. Like Carmen and Roberto, they start their own families far from any relatives. ■

THINK IT THROUGH

What Kind of Family?

Directions: Read each sentence (or sentences) below carefully. Decide whether each describes a nuclear family or an extended family, and then circle the correct response. The first one is done for you.

1. Carol Smith lives in Columbus with her parents.

   The Smiths are a/an (**nuclear**/*extended*) family.

2. There are forty-two members in the Sosa family. They all live in Pittsburgh, and they see each other often.

   The Sosas are a/an (*nuclear*/*extended*) family.

3. Ken Lucio lives in Dallas with his ten-year-old son.

   Ken Lucio and his son are a/an (*nuclear*/*extended*) family.

4. The Millers own a farm in Wisconsin. Their three sons and their sons' families all live and work on the farm.

   The Millers are a/an (*nuclear*/*extended*) family.

5. According to the reading on page 4, this type of family was affected by changes in transportation and industry in the early 1900s. (*nuclear*/*extended*)

6. Name the members of your nuclear family.

   _____
   _____

7. Name some members of your extended family.

   _____
   _____
   _____
   _____

ANOTHER LOOK

Imagine you are moving away from your nuclear family to start a new life.

Think about the questions below and jot down brief answers to them.

1. Where do you think you might go? _____
   _____
   _____

2. What kind of work would you try to find? _____
   _____
   _____

3. How would you go about finding a new job? _____
   _____
   _____

4. Would there be members of your extended family nearby to give you support? _____
   _____
   _____

VOCABULARY

extended family
a large family group made up of parents, children, and all their relatives

industry
any business that makes products or provides services

nuclear family
a small family group made up of parents and their children

relatives
family members; people who are related to you

society
people who live together in a group

structure
the way something is built or arranged

transportation
any means of travel from one place to another ■

VOCABULARY PRACTICE

Part 1: Work with Family Terms

Directions: Match each word on the left with its correct set of examples on the right by writing the correct letter on each line. The first one is done for you.

_b_   1. nuclear family
____ 2. industry
____ 3. society
____ 4. extended family
____ 5. transportation

(a) Americans, Europeans, Asians
(b) parents, children
(c) car, boat, plane
(d) factories, shops
(e) parents, children, relatives

Part 2: More Than One Meaning

Directions: As you may know, some words have more than one meaning. All dictionaries list different meanings of a word. Look at the basic definition of *structure* in the vocabulary list. Then read the sentences below to see how this word can be used in different ways. Match each definition on the right with the correct sentence on the left. If you need to, check a dictionary to see how the different meanings of *structure* are listed.

____ 1. Every essay should have an organized structure.

____ 2. There is a crack in the structure of that bridge.

____ 3. Some scientists study the structure of plants.

(a) the way parts and particles form living things
(b) the way ideas are organized on paper
(c) the way something is built, or constructed

WORD ATTACK

It's a Syllable!

Say the word *son* aloud, and tap your finger once as you say it. You should hear one beat in the word *son*. Now say the word *children*, and tap your finger with each beat. You should hear two beats in this word.

How many beats do you hear in the word *family*? _____

If you hear three beats, you are right.

Each beat in a word is called a **syllable**. Words can have one syllable, such as *son* and *dad*. Or they can have several syllables, such as *family* (fam/i/ly) and *grandparent* (grand/par/ent). The slash marks show each beat, or syllable.

Say the following words aloud. Then write the number of syllables in each word on the blank lines.

1. aunt _____

2. industry _____

3. father _____

You were correct if you wrote 1 beside *aunt*, 3 beside *industry* (in/dus/try), and 2 beside *father* (fa/ther).

PRACTICE

Directions: Say each of the following words aloud, and tap your finger with each beat. Listen closely to the syllables in each, and decide whether the word has one, two, or three syllables. Write each word in the correct column, then draw a line between the beats you hear. One is done for you as an example.

love	extended	Carmen
parent	relative	mom
nuclear	uncle	home

One Syllable　　**Two Syllables**　　**Three Syllables**

　　　　　　　　　　　　　　　　　　　ex/tend/ed

7

FOR FUN
A Family Tree

Do you know anything about your great-grandmother or great-great-grandfather? Do you know where they were born? What kind of life they had?

People often gather facts about their ancestors, or long-ago relatives, and make family trees. A family tree shows the names, birth dates, and marriages of the people who made your family what it is today.

Talk with your family and see how much you can discover about your ancestors. Then make your own family tree below.

Write the name and the date each person was born in the box. If a person has died, also write the date he or she died.

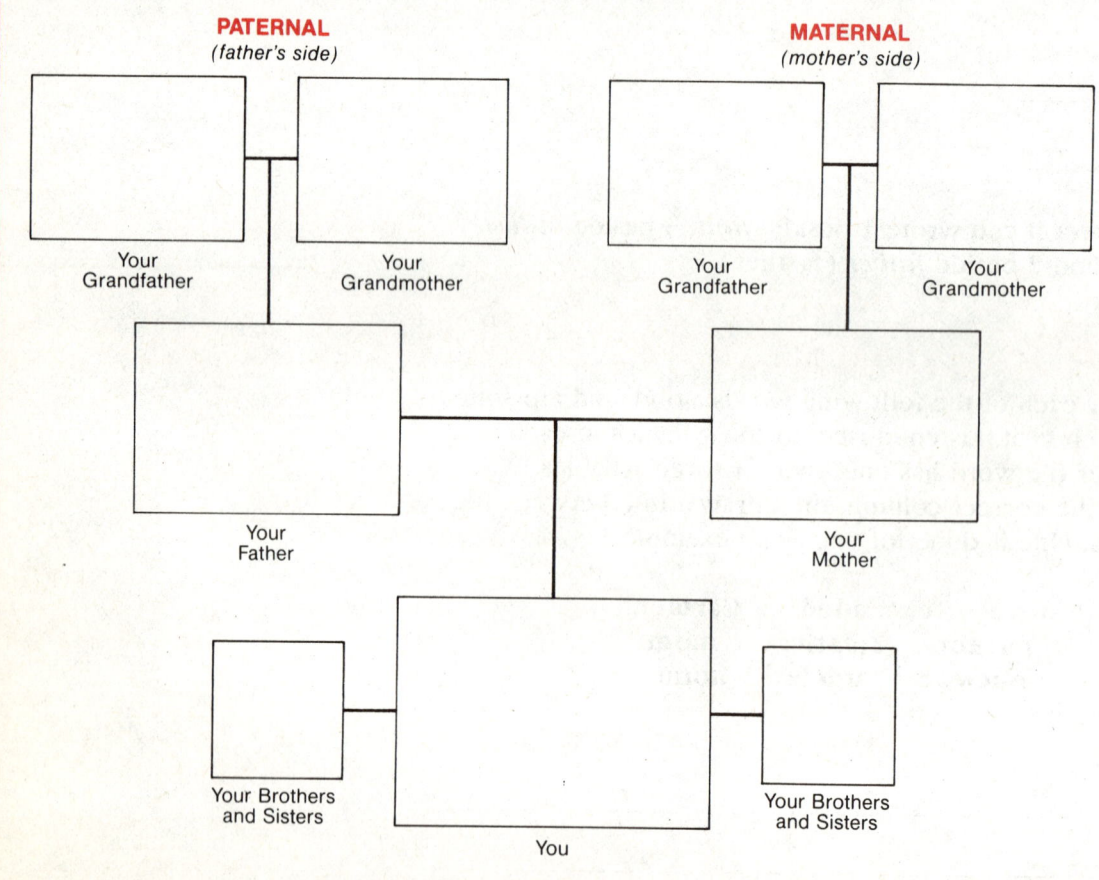

8

Single-Parent Dad

Writing down thoughts and ideas in a journal can be a good way to sort through problems. In this journal, a single-parent father tells what happened to his family during one week in May.

MAY 23

Ann, my three-year-old daughter, has to have heart surgery next Monday. One of the valves in her heart isn't working. Since I'll be with Ann all the time, my six-year-old son Joe will have to stay with friends for one or two weeks. When I told Joe this, he looked scared.

MAY 24

My boss is letting me work from 4 P.M. to midnight. This way, I can be with Ann most of the day and then work while she sleeps.

"I know what it's like raising children on your own," my boss said. "When my husband and I divorced, I got the kids. The first year was the toughest."

I didn't think I could manage alone when Agnes died. I still don't.

MAY 25

Joe ran away after school today. Our friends, Tim and Karen, said he had been crying all afternoon. He told them that his mother was gone and his father and sister were leaving him, too.

I found Joe at about 7:00 P.M. He was a few blocks from our house. I didn't know whether to punish him or not. After I saw how unhappy he was, I knew I couldn't.

Why do children enjoy times like these with their parents?

MAY 26

Joe and I spent the afternoon at the park. I think he really enjoyed the attention.

As soon as Ann is well, I'll spend more time like this with Joe. I want to figure out what kind of parent I am and what kind of parent Joe needs right now.

SKILL BUILD

Details in the Newspaper

In the journal you just read, the father gave important facts about each day's event.

Like journal entries, newspaper stories give important facts about a day's events. Often, the first paragraph in a newspaper story gives you each detail you need to understand it.

Most reporters write their stories by answering the **five W questions**. Read the first paragraph of a newspaper story below. Then answer the questions that follow.

Doctor's Advice—for Free

To celebrate Child's Week, doctors in the San Bruno area will give free advice to parents. The doctors will be at radio station KDAN from 2-4 P.M., August 8-12. Call them at 555-9291.

1. Who is this story about? _____

2. What are the doctors going to do? _____

3. Where will the doctors be? _____

4. When will the radio program take place? _____

5. Why will the doctors give free advice? _____

Your answers should be similar to these:

1. The story is about doctors in the San Bruno area.
2. The doctors will give free advice about children's health.
3. The doctors will be at radio station KDAN in San Bruno.
4. The radio program will take place from 2-4 P.M., August 8-12.
5. They will give free advice to help celebrate Child's Week.

By answering the five Ws, you have learned important details about the news story. The rest of the story will give more specific details about the five Ws.

POINT TO REMEMBER

Most newspaper articles tell *who*, *what*, *when*, *where*, and *why* in the first paragraph or two.

DETAILS PRACTICE

Directions: Below are the beginnings of several newspaper stories. Read them carefully, then answer the questions that follow.

1. Janesville Care House, a new daycare center for children ages one to five, opened Monday, September 6. Owned by Mabel Woods, the center is located at 15 River Street.

    "Janesville may be a small town," Mabel said, "but many of our families have two working parents. These parents need good daycare for their children."

    a. Who is the new center for? _____
    b. What is the owner's name? _____
    c. When did the center open? _____
    d. Where is the center located? _____
    e. Why is daycare important in Janesville? _____

2. City College will offer a parenting class in the fall. Dr. Susan Kubota and Dr. Gene Wong, child psychologists, will teach the eight-week course.

    "Nobody is born with parenting skills," says Dr. Kubota. "That's why this class will be so helpful."

    a. Who is named in the story? _____
    b. What class is being offered? _____
    c. When will the course begin? _____
    d. Where will the course be taught? _____
    e. Why will this class be helpful? _____

3. Concerned with the number of teenage alcoholics in this country, Youth Group, Inc., took a survey last May. The group traveled across the country and talked with more than 125,000 children about alcohol and their abuse of this drug.

    a. Who took the survey? _____
    b. What did they talk to children about? _____
    c. When did the survey take place? _____
    d. Where did they take the survey? _____
    e. Why did they take the survey? _____

ONE MORE STEP

Newspapers often print announcements about important events such as births and marriages. On the lines below, describe an event that happened in your family recently. (Or find a real announcement in your local newspaper.)

Who is the announcement about?
_____
_____
_____

What happened? _____
_____
_____
_____

When did it happen?
_____
_____
_____

Where did it happen?
_____
_____
_____

Why did it happen?
_____
_____
_____

Parenting Styles

Whom do you think of when you hear the word *teacher*? Your best—or worst—instructor in school? An older sister or friend? Your parents?

We don't usually think of parents as teachers, but parents are often the most important teachers children ever have.

Parents help teach their children how to walk, talk, play, and eat. They try to teach children the **values** that will help them grow into responsible adults.

Raising children, or **parenting**, is not easy. It is a skill that must be learned. Often, parenting is learned through **trial and error**. Sometimes it's learned from asking the advice of friends or other parents.

Do you know some parents who are strict and others who let their children do almost anything? If so, you have seen some of the ways that parents handle children. Even though every parent is different, **experts** agree that there are three basic **parenting styles**:

- **Autocratic** parents **dictate** how their children behave by setting firm rules.

- **Authoritative** parents allow their children freedom to explore the world, but they also set fair limits.

- **Permissive** parents allow children to do and say almost anything. Such parents rarely make rules.

How would each type of parent handle this problem?

Nick, who is seven, wants to go outside. He puts on his favorite sweater. His father sees that the sweater is not warm enough.

An autocratic parent would order Nick to put on a warmer sweater. If Nick refused to change, he would be punished.

An authoritative father would explain to Nick why he needs a warmer sweater and would make sure Nick decides that a warmer sweater is better.

A permissive parent might tell Nick that he needs a warmer sweater but would let him decide whether or not to change.

Of course, all parents act differently on different days, depending on their moods and the child's needs. No parent uses only one style all of the time. ■

How should this father handle the situation?

THINK IT THROUGH

A Parent's Life

Directions: Circle the answer that completes each sentence correctly.

1. The first, and often most important, teachers in a child's life are his/her

    (a) experts
    (b) sisters
    (c) parents
    (d) aunts and uncles

2. Raising children is also called

    (a) parenting
    (b) trial and error
    (c) asking for advice
    (d) style

3. An *autocratic* parent would

    (a) let children watch as much TV as they want
    (b) set a strict time limit on TV watching
    (c) work out a TV schedule with the children
    (d) only own a black-and-white TV

4. Joel's parents tell him that he must be in by 10 P.M. Joel, who is fourteen years old, shows up at 1 A.M. His parents don't criticize or punish him. Joel's parents are

    (a) autocratic
    (b) authoritative
    (c) permissive
    (d) crazy

ANOTHER LOOK

Read the paragraph below, then answer the questions that follow.

It is 10:00 P.M. on a Tuesday night. The Moore house is again filled with the sounds of fighting. Maria Moore, a sophomore in high school, wants to go out with friends that her mother and stepfather do not like. Maria warns her parents that if they say no again, she will leave home for good.

1. What is the conflict, or problem, between Maria and her parents?

   _____
   _____
   _____
   _____
   _____

2. Imagine that you are Maria's mother or stepfather. What would you say to her?

   _____
   _____
   _____
   _____
   _____
   _____
   _____

VOCABULARY

authoritative
sets rules but also allows freedom

autocratic
sets strict rules

dictate
to speak or act with great power and control

experts
people who have special knowledge in a certain area

parenting
the raising of children

parenting style
the way a parent raises his or her children

permissive
allows freedom with few rules

trial and error
finding the best way to do something by trying one method, then another

values
a person's beliefs about what is important in life

VOCABULARY PRACTICE

Part 1: Identify Parenting Styles

Directions: Match each quote on the left with the parenting style it describes. Write the correct letter in the space provided.

_____ 1. "My parents are strict. They set rules for me to follow."

_____ 2. "My mom and dad don't set many rules. I can do whatever I want."

_____ 3. "My parents set some rules, but they also let me make decisions."

(a) authoritative
(b) permissive
(c) autocratic

Part 2: More Than One Meaning

Directions: Look up the words *style* and *value* in the dictionary. Notice that each word may have more than one meaning. Then decide which word correctly completes each sentence below.

style   value

1. Sandy bought a magazine to see the new _____ in swimsuits.

2. What will the _____ of the house be after 25 years?

3. Some people _____ good health over money.

4. This student's writing _____ is very simple.

5. Even though that woman's speech lasted an hour, she had nothing of _____ to say.

14

WORD ATTACK

Compound Words

Step and *mother*. When you put these two words together, what one word can you form?

Together, these words form the word *stepmother*. Stepmother is a **compound word**. Compound words are made up of two smaller words. Here are some other common compound words:

in + to = into

some + thing = something

book + store = bookstore

in + side = inside

some + body = somebody

air + plane = airplane

PRACTICE

Directions: Form at least *four* compound words by putting together the words listed below. Then write sentences using each of the compound words you formed. One is done for you. (Hint: a total of seven words is possible.)

	grand	step	sitter
baby	parent	father	daughter

1. *grandfather*
   My grandfather owned a dairy farm.

2. _____

3. _____

4. _____

5. _____

15

FOR FUN

Keeping Dates Straight

Whether or not you're a parent, you know how hard it can be to remember dates, times, and places.

To keep better track of dates and times, use a calendar like the one below. This calendar belongs to Cheri Bookman, a divorced mother of three. What is Cheri doing on June 2? _____

If you said that Cheri is taking Kevin to the doctor at 2 P.M., you're right.

Cheri is also going to the events below. Write each event and its time on the correct date.

- Family trip to Sea Show, June 11, 10 A.M.
- Parenting class, June 7 and 14, 7:30 P.M.
- Wedding on June 22, 8 P.M.

When can Cheri go to a 7:00 P.M. baseball game? The games are taking place on June 7, 14, 21, and 22. Find the one date she can go to the game, then schedule it on the calendar.

June

S	M	T	W	T	F	S
	1	2 *Kevin to doctor 2 p.m.*	3	4	5	6	7
8	9	10	11	12	13	14
15	16	17	18	19	20	21
22	23	24	25	26	27	28
29	30					

Married or Single?

CARYL SMITH
age 41, married

I only know what marriage is like. Dave and I got married right after high school. We have four kids. We've always had to compromise on how we spend our money and what we do with our free time. I guess that's part of marriage.

MARIA PADERNA
age 21, single

I like being single and supporting myself. I'm doing things that I've always wanted to do. Last September, I took a train across Canada. This spring, I'm going rafting in the Grand Canyon. To me, being married means paying a mortgage and raising children. I'm not ready for that.

LEO WASHINGTON
age 29, single

I'd like to get married in a year or two. Oh, there are a lot of things I like about being single. It can also be very lonely, though. When I'm married, I'll have someone to share my life with. We can make a home and start a family together.

JIM YOUNGBLOOD
age 33, single

The way I see it, being single is better. I can do things that I couldn't do if I were married. Being single, I can go to Brazil, climb Mt. Everest, or go skydiving. I only have to worry about myself, not a wife and kids. Marriage is not my kind of adventure yet. ■

SKILL BUILD

Please Restate That!

- Life is nicer when you can share it with someone you love.
- It's better to spend your life with a person you really care about.

Even though these two sentences look different, they have the same meaning. They use different words to express the same thought. Saying the same thing in different words is called **restating**. Any time you tell a friend about an argument you had or what happened in a movie, you are restating.

In the previous story, Jim Youngblood tells how he feels about marriage. Read the sentences below again, and think about how you could restate them.

> The way I see it, being single is better. I can do things that I couldn't do if I were married. Being single, I can go to Brazil, climb Mt. Everest, or go skydiving.

Here is one way to restate these sentences:

> Jim Youngblood likes being single. He thinks that if he were married, he couldn't travel or do exciting things like climb mountains.

Now try restating the statements below.

> I only have to worry about myself, not a wife and kids. Marriage is not my kind of adventure yet.

_____

_____

Have your teacher or a friend check your response. You may have written something like, "Jim Youngblood does not want to worry about a family. He is not ready for marriage yet."

▼ **POINT TO REMEMBER**

One way to make sure you understand something is to restate it, or put it in your own words.

RESTATING PRACTICE

Part 1

Directions: The sentences on the right are restatements of the sentences on the left. Put the letter of each sentence on the right by the sentence it restates. The first one is done for you.

__C__ 1. Lucy and Tony Coe were married in 1988.

_____ 2. They started to argue on their honeymoon, and they never stopped.

_____ 3. Their friends decided that Lucy and Tony enjoy arguing.

_____ 4. Lucy and Tony got a divorce last week.

(a) They have been fighting ever since their honeymoon.

(b) The Coes just ended their marriage.

(c) Lucy and Tony got married in the late 1980s.

(d) Lucy and Tony argue so much that people think they like it.

Part 2

Directions: Read the following statements. Then, on the lines below, restate each sentence.

1. Curtis and Lisa dated for five years and then broke up.

   _____
   _____

2. When his parents' divorce became final, Henry vowed never to marry.

   _____
   _____

3. Madge and Harold got married last week in Detroit City Hall.

   _____
   _____

ONE MORE STEP

Today, many couples write their own marriage vows. Read the traditional vows that follow, and think about how you might restate them. On the lines below, write your own vows.

I take you to be my wedded spouse to have and to hold from this day forward. For better, or worse; for richer, or poorer; in sickness and in health; to love and to cherish; till death do us part.

_____
_____
_____
_____
_____
_____
_____
_____
_____
_____
_____
_____

Marriage Trends

As you know from reading about their lives, Maria Paderna, Leo Washington, and Jim Youngblood are all single. If they get married this year, or even if they stay single, they will affect the marriage **rate** in America.

The marriage rate tells how many Americans out of every 1,000 get married each year. If the marriage rate is 9, then 9 out of every 1,000 Americans got married that year.

Look at the **graph** below. This graph shows the marriage rates from 1910 to 1985. What was the marriage rate in 1920? To find out, first find the bar with the years across it. This is called the *horizontal axis*. Now put your finger on the spot that says '20 (for the year 1920).

Next, move your finger straight up from the year 1920 until you hit a dot. This dot is across from the number 12 on the *vertical axis*, or up-and-down bar. You now know that the marriage rate for 1920 was 12. That year, 12 out of every 1,000 Americans got married.

Now look at how the dots rise and fall across the graph. This rising and falling is called the marriage **curve**. The curve shows you that the marriage rate rose and fell two times between 1910 and 1940. It dropped to its lowest point in 1960. After rising again, it leveled off between 1970 and 1980.

Has the marriage rate **increased** or **decreased** since 1980? It has decreased, or fallen. Why do you think fewer people are getting married each year? **Researchers** say that this **trend**, or pattern, is due to two factors.

First, people have been marrying for the first time when they are a few years older. Also, some women are **postponing**, or putting off, marriage until they have started their careers. They want to focus on their work for a few years before adding the responsibility of marriage.

Researchers believe that the trend of marrying later will result in fewer divorces. They think that people who are in their late twenties know more about what they want in a marriage partner than people in their early twenties do. ■

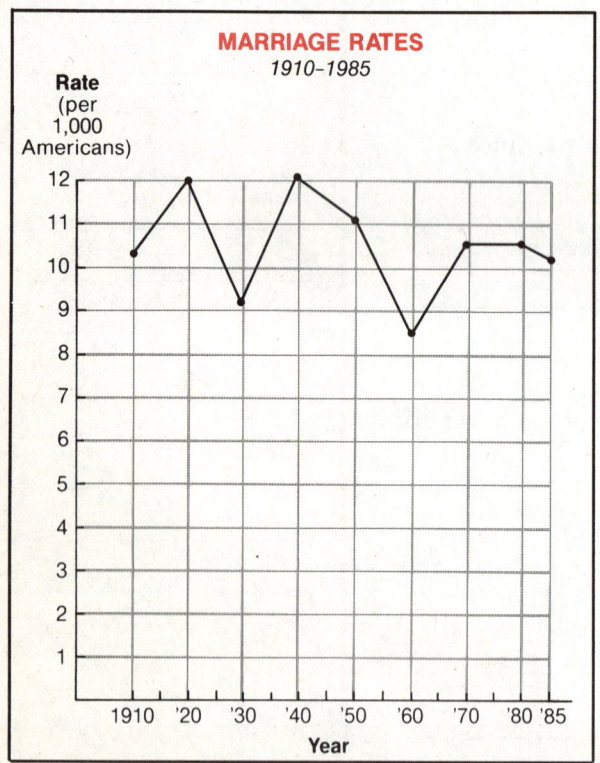

THINK IT THROUGH

Graph It!

Directions: The statements below refer to the passage that you just read. Read the details of each statement carefully. If the statement is true, write *T*. If the statement is false, write *F*.

_____ 1. The marriage rate for 1984 tells how many people were divorced that year.

_____ 2. Men and women today are marrying at a younger age.

_____ 3. Researchers believe that the trend of marrying later will result in more divorces.

Questions 4-9 refer to the graph on page 20.

_____ 4. The marriage rate was at its lowest in 1960.

_____ 5. The marriage rate in 1985 was lower than in 1980.

_____ 6. The marriage rate decreased from 1960 to 1970.

_____ 7. The horizontal axis shows the years 1910-1985.

_____ 8. The vertical axis shows the numbers 1-12.

_____ 9. You can tell from this graph that the marriage rate for 1900 was 9.

ANOTHER LOOK

Before the 1970s, many unhappy couples stayed together for the sake of their children. Now, though, many couples get a divorce instead. They believe that their unhappy marriage is more stressful for children than a divorce.

What do you think? Are children hurt more by an unhappy marriage or by a divorce? On the lines below, first write your opinion. Then write two reasons that support your opinion.

Opinion

_____
_____
_____

Reasons

1. _____
_____
_____
_____
_____

2. _____
_____
_____
_____
_____

VOCABULARY

curve
the rising and falling of rates on a graph

decrease
to become less, or smaller

graph
a drawing that shows the relationship between two or more things

increase
to become greater, or larger

postpone
to put off, or delay

rate
a quantity or amount; for example, the unemployment rate

researcher
a person who gathers information about a subject

trend
a pattern or development ■

VOCABULARY PRACTICE

Part 1: Marriage Rate Terms
Directions: Complete each sentence using the correct word below.

    curve   decrease   increase
       rate   researcher

1. If fewer people are married in 1990 than in 1987, the marriage _____ for 1990 will be less than for 1987.

2. Ralph works as a _____ for a company that studies trends in advertising.

3. If there are fewer divorces this year, the divorce rate will _____.

4. If there are more marriages, the marriage rate will _____.

5. The _____ on that divorce graph shows that the divorce rate has been falling.

Part 2: More Than One Meaning
Directions: You have learned one meaning for *rate* and *trend*. Check the dictionary for other meanings, then decide which word correctly completes each sentence.

       rate   trend

1. The newest fashion _____ is shorter skirts.

2. The mortgage _____ for new homes seems to go up each year.

3. The judges will _____ the singers from first place to fourth place.

4. One current _____ in rock music is benefit concerts for the hungry and the homeless.

WORD ATTACK

End It!

Milton is **looking** for a wife. He wants to find her **quickly**. He wants to stay married **longer** than he did the first time. That was the **shortest** marriage ever—only two weeks!

Look at the words in **boldface** type above. Each of them has two parts—a main word and a **suffix**, or ending. What is the main word in *looking*? _____
You're correct if you said *look*.
What is the suffix, or ending, in *looking*? _____
You're right if you said *ing*.
Now take a look at each of the main words and endings from the story above.

> looking = look + ing
> quickly = quick + ly
> longer = long + er
> shortest = short + est

These four endings—*-ing*, *-ly*, *-er*, and *-est*—are common endings. If you look for them as you read something new, words that look hard to read will be easier. Just break them down into two parts—the main word and the suffix.

PRACTICE

Directions: Complete each sentence below by adding the correct suffix—*-ing*, *-ly*, *-er*, or *-est*—to each word. The first one is done for you.

1. Walt is at the hospital look__ing__ at his newborn son.

2. Walt's wife Jean is stand_____ beside him.

3. Even though Walt is the young_____ in his family, he already has a wife and child.

4. Jean is even young_____ than Walt. She is 21.

5. They have wise_____ decided to save money for the baby's education.

FOR FUN

Crossword Puzzle

Directions: Use the words in the box to complete each sentence. Then complete the crossword puzzle below. The first one is done for you.

children   wedding   vows
single   love

Down

1. Maria bought Anthony a gold watch. I think she is in _love_ with him.

3. There will be 200 guests at my son's _____ next Saturday.

Across

2. "Did you cry when you said your wedding _____?"

4. "I have six sons and five daughters. Do you have any _____?"

5. "Most of my friends are married, but I'm still _____."

24

ISSUES

Does One Vote Make a Difference?

Scene: In front of a supermarket, VICKI, a 34-year-old woman, is registering people to vote. A 50-year-old man walks by.

VICKI: Good afternoon, sir. Are you registered to vote?

CARL: No, not since I moved.

VICKI: Would you like to register?

CARL: No, thank you. I stopped voting ten years ago. *(keeps walking)*

VICKI: *(calls out)* That's your right, sir. Do you mind telling me why you stopped voting?

CARL: *(walks back to VICKI)* I got angry. I didn't like the way politicians ran the government, and I didn't like the people who were running for office. Also, I didn't think that my vote would make a difference. So why bother?

VICKI: I used to think that way, too. Then someone pointed out to me that politicians hold public offices. They represent us. If politicians want to stay in office, they must listen to the people. Of course, that means we have to tell them what we think.

CARL: Well, you have a point there.

VICKI: I'm 34. I could have started voting when I was 18, but I didn't. In fact, I voted for the first time last year.

CARL: *(sits down at VICKI's table)* What made you start voting?

VICKI: Proposition X in last year's election. The city wanted to sell public land to a developer. The developer was going to build 80 homes but sell only 20 of them to low-income and middle-income families.

CARL: Yes, I remember that issue. I didn't think the developer's idea was fair.

VICKI: Neither did I. So I registered to vote. For once, I wanted my voice heard. I even volunteered to work on the "Say NO to Prop X" campaign.

CARL: You won, hands down.

Registering to vote takes only a few minutes.

VICKI: Yes, we did. City leaders heard us loud and clear. Here, take this registration form. If you decide to fill it out, mail it directly to this address.

CARL: Thanks. I'll think about what you've said. *(He takes the sheet and walks away.)*

VICKI: Thank you . . . Hello, ma'am. Are you registered to vote? ■

SKILL BUILD

Summarizing

After Carl talked to Vicki, he went home and told his wife about the conversation. Instead of trying to repeat every word, though, he gave his wife a summary of his talk with Vicki. A **summary** is a short description that covers all the important facts. Here is what Carl told his wife:

> "At the supermarket, I ran into a young lady who was registering people to vote. She gave me some good reasons to start voting again."

To summarize, first find all the important details. Then describe those details in one or two short statements.

Read the facts below, then write a summary of them.

1. Carl didn't like how politicians ran the government.
2. He didn't like the people running for public office.
3. He didn't think that his vote would make a difference.

_____
_____
_____

Your summary could be something like this: Carl stopped voting because he lost faith in the voting system. Read the details below, then write a summary of them.

1. Politicians must listen to what the people say.
2. The people must tell their leaders what they think and want.
3. Politicians must act on behalf of the people.

_____
_____
_____

Here is one possible summary: Politicians and the people must communicate well.

▼ POINT TO REMEMBER

To make a summary, describe all the important facts or points in one or two general sentences.

SUMMARIZING PRACTICE

Directions: Read each point below. Then write a one-sentence summary on each poster.

1.
   - Ben Gonzalez has been a businessman all his life.
   - He supported the decrease in the business tax.
   - He will make sure the Business Center is built.

GONZALEZ FOR MAYOR

_____
_____
_____
_____
_____

2.
   - Molly Heller believes that schools should offer after-school daycare.
   - She believes in giving new mothers one full year before they must decide whether or not to come back to work.
   - She believes that low-cost health clinics for the entire family should be available.

HELLER FOR CONGRESS

_____
_____
_____
_____
_____

ONE MORE STEP

Think of an office that you would like to be elected to. For example, you might want to be president of a club or chairman of the school board. What qualities or experiences do you have that might help you win the office?

Write three of these qualities or facts below. Then write a summary describing yourself on another sheet of paper.

Facts about yourself:

1. _____
   _____
   _____
   _____

2. _____
   _____
   _____
   _____

3. _____
   _____
   _____
   _____

Registering to Vote

In the United States, people have the right to **vote**, or choose their government leaders. They also have the right to vote on important issues such as raising taxes. Voting is a right that people don't have in some other countries.

On **election** days, registered voters go to **polling places** to vote. A polling place can be a school, church, apartment building, or any other neighborhood place. Election judges are there to show voters what to do.

Qualifications to vote in the United States are simple.

- You must be a U.S. **citizen**.

- You must be at least 18 years old by the next election.

- You must not be serving a sentence on a **felony** charge.

- You must have lived in your state for a certain number of days. Every state has a different requirement.

If you meet all of these conditions, then you can **register** to vote. When you register, you must fill out a form called an **affidavit**. You can get an affidavit from your county's Registrar of Voters or Board of Elections office. You can also get one at your local post office, or at voter registration tables in shopping centers and other public places.

When you have completed the affidavit, send or take it to the office that registers voters. The office will make sure your name is put on the state's list of voters. Anytime you move, even if it's just next door, you must fill out an affidavit.

Once your name is registered, you will be sent a voter registration card. It will say that you are a qualified voter in your state. You can now exercise your right to vote. ■

Each voting booth contains simple instructions on how to cast your vote.

THINK IT THROUGH

Signing Up

Directions: Answer the questions below. If you need to, refer back to the passage on page 28.

1. How old must you be in order to vote?
_____

2. Where could you pick up an affidavit in your community?
_____

3. How will you know when you are registered to vote?
_____
_____

4. Todd just moved from 241 Gale Street to 248 Gale Street. What should he do to stay registered to vote?
_____
_____
_____

5. Layla is 17 years old. Last week, she became a U.S. citizen. She has lived in Texas for five years, and she has never been arrested.

Is Layla qualified to register to vote? Why or why not?
_____
_____
_____

ANOTHER LOOK

Suppose the United States changed its laws, and citizens had to pay a tax of $20 in order to vote for a new president.

1. Who would this tax affect most?
_____
_____
_____
_____

2. How would it affect them?
_____
_____
_____
_____

3. Why do you think this tax is now against the law?
_____
_____
_____
_____

VOCABULARY

affidavit
a statement in writing that a person swears is true

citizen
a person who is a member of a country by birth or by choice and who is granted the rights of that nation

election
an event in which voters choose political leaders

felony
a serious crime, such as murder or robbery

polling place
neighborhood place, such as a school or church, where people go to vote

qualification
a condition that must be met to do something

register
to add your name to your state's list of voters

vote
to choose between candidates and issues in an election

VOCABULARY PRACTICE

Part 1: Work with Voting Terms

Directions: Complete the sentences below. Use the words below to fill in each blank.

affidavit   citizen   election
qualification   register   polling place

1. Lamar went to the _____ at 6:00 A.M to vote.

2. Mr. Russo was sworn in as a U.S. _____ last month.

3. Registered voters must fill out a new _____ whenever they move to a new address.

4. After winning last year's _____, the new mayor kept his promises.

5. One _____ for voting is that you must be a U.S. citizen.

6. The Democratic Club will _____ people to vote this Sunday at the Fast Stop Market.

Part 2: More Than One Meaning

Directions: Fill in each blank below with the word *register* or *issue*. Think about the different meanings each word has.

register   issue

1. The storekeeper counted the money in the cash _____.

2. The Balbonis went down to city hall to _____ their baby's birth.

3. The city will _____ new parking permits today.

4. The candidates agreed on the _____ of less pay for elected officials.

5. Did you get your new _____ of *Time*?

6. Debra will _____ this letter with the post office because it is so important.

WORD ATTACK

More Endings

Each word in **dark type** below is made up of two parts. Each has a main word, like *care* or *hat*, and a suffix, like *-ful* or *-less*.

- Leticia is a **careful** driver. (*care + ful*)
- The farmworker was **hatless** in the hot sun. (*hat + less*)
- The candidate voted for **himself**. (*him + self*)
- Jo bought the sports **equipment** on sale. (*equip + ment*)
- The father's **illness** was hard on the family. (*ill + ness*)

PRACTICE

Part 1: Work with One Suffix

Directions: Each of the sentences below contains an incomplete word. Add the correct suffix from the box to make the words and the sentences complete. The first one is done for you.

    -ful   -less   -ment   -ness   -self

1. Did you fix the air conditioner your *self* ?

2. The car's headlights shone through the dark _____ .

3. Angela is a master _____ dancer.

4. His father scolded him count _____ times.

Part 2: Work with Two Suffixes

- Roberto's **willingness** to work hard got him the job.

How many suffixes can you find in the word *willingness*? _____
You're right if you see two suffixes: *-ing* and *-ness*. Even though a long word like *willingness* looks hard to read, it can be broken down into small, easy-to-read parts: will + ing + ness.
Directions: Complete the sentences below by adding either *-ly* or *-ness* to the incomplete word. The first one is done for you.

1. The hopeless *ness* of Jan's problem made her cry.

2. The father smiling _____ thought of his new baby.

3. Warren faithful _____ worked for the mayor on election day.

4. Because of his forgetful _____ , Bo didn't register to vote.

FOR FUN

Fill It Out

When you register to vote, you must write this information on your affidavit:

- Your *full* name
- Your home address. If the address where you receive your mail is different, write that address too.
- Your date of birth and birthplace

Before you sign your affidavit, check it over. Make sure the information is correct. Also, make sure you understand each of the questions. If you don't, ask someone for help.

Fill out the sample affidavit below. It shows the kind of information that you must complete on a real one.

```
(check one)      ____Mr.   ____Mrs.   ____Miss   ____Ms.
1. Name _____
         first            middle              last
2. Residence address _____
                    street and number    apartment number
   _____
      city         county         state         zip code
3. Mailing address if different from residence
   _____
   _____
4. Date of birth _____
5. Birthplace _____
              name of U.S. state or foreign country
6. Political Party (check one):
   ____ American Independent Party
   ____ Democratic Party
   ____ Peace and Freedom Party
   ____ Republican Party
   ____ Decline to state
   ____ Other _____
I am a citizen of the United States. I will be at least 18 years old by the next election. I am not in prison on a felony charge. I swear that everything on this affidavit is true.
Signature _____ Date _____
```

SAMPLE

My Right to Read

Dear Editor,

Last month, six Lakeview citizens formed a group called "Protect Our Children." The members have made a list of 100 books in the children's section of the library that they believe are harmful to children. They want those 100 books to be removed.

Many of the 100 books are about real-life problems such as prejudice and drug abuse. Some of the group members admitted that they have not read all the books. They made up their minds just from hearing what other people said.

Our children see that parents do not have the answer to every problem in life. My husband and I remember that young children have thoughts and beliefs of their own.

I know that the books I want my children to read may not be the same books other parents want for their children. In the United States, though, people have the right to read whatever they want. The Constitution gives us this freedom.

I do not mind if this group speaks out about books they think are harmful. That is their right. This group cannot ban books

Parents can encourage their children to read by taking them to the library.

One book that the group wants to ban is a collection of stories, poems, and songs about families. Why do they want to ban this book? One member says that parents look silly and confused in some stories. Another member thinks that the book makes children seem smarter than their parents.

My husband and I often read this book with our children. We find nothing harmful about the stories. In fact, we think the stories help us get along better as a family.

from the public library, however. They cannot tell people what to read. They can ban the 100 books from their own homes, but not from my home or my library.

Sincerely yours,

Jennifer Ergina

Jennifer Ergina
Lakeview

SKILL BUILD

Finding a Main Idea

Every paragraph has a **main idea**. Often, this main idea is stated directly in the first or last sentence of a paragraph. Read the paragraph below, and look for the main idea.

<u>One book that the group wants to ban is a collection of poems, stories, and songs about families.</u> Why do they want to ban this book? One member thinks that parents seem silly and confused in some stories. Another member thinks the book makes children seem smarter than their parents.

In this paragraph, the main idea is stated in the first sentence: "One book that the group wants to ban is a collection of poems, stories, and songs about families." The other sentences in the paragraph all give supporting details that tell why the group wants to ban this book.

To find the main idea in any paragraph, ask yourself this question: "What one thought or idea do all the other sentences describe or support?"

The main idea is not always given in the first or last sentence of a paragraph. It may be stated in the second, third, or fourth sentence. Read the paragraph below. Underline the sentence that states the main idea.

I know that the books I want my children to read may not be the same books other parents want for their children. In the United States, though, people have the right to read whatever they want. The Constitution gives us this freedom.

Here, the main idea is given in the second sentence: "In the United States, though, people have the right to read whatever they want." The other sentences contain details which support this main idea.

▼ POINT TO REMEMBER

Every paragraph has one main idea. To find the main idea, ask yourself, "What one thought or idea do the other details in the paragraph support?"

MAIN IDEA PRACTICE

Directions: Read each paragraph below. Draw a line under the sentence that states the main idea. Hint: The main ideas below will be stated in the first or the last sentence.

1. Our country's first constitution was called the Articles of Confederation. It was approved by the thirteen states in 1781. The Articles of Confederation gave the states more power than the federal government. For example, each state could make its own money and place taxes on goods from another state.

2. Because each state could make its own money, there were many different kinds of money. As a result, the money was often worthless. Taxes and prices were too high. States even fought each other. The national leaders couldn't do anything because they only had the power to advise the states. For these reasons, many Americans were unhappy with the Articles of Confederation.

3. In May 1787, twelve of the thirteen states sent representatives to a convention in Philadelphia, PA. Their job was to revise, or make changes in, the Articles of Confederation. Instead, they decided to make a new constitution. They talked about how the federal government in Washington should be run. They discussed how each state should be represented. By December, the delegates had written and signed a new constitution.

4. The U.S. Constitution opens with a short preamble, or introduction. The preamble states that the Constitution is made by and for the people. After the preamble are the seven articles. The articles point out the different powers of the federal government and the states. After the articles are the amendments. These are laws that have been added over the years to make the Constitution stronger and more modern. These three parts make up the structure of the U.S. Constitution—the preamble, articles, and amendments.

ONE MORE STEP

Do you think the president is a strong leader? Why or why not?

On the lines below, write a paragraph giving your opinion and your reasons for it. Make sure you have one sentence that states the main idea.

The Bill of Rights

When the U.S. **Constitution** was written in 1787, leaders wanted to be sure that it would be able to change with the times. So they decided that future leaders could amend the Constitution—that is, they could add or take out laws. Since 1787, 26 **amendments** have been added to our Constitution.

The best-known amendments are the first 10. These are called the Bill of Rights. They state the basic rights and freedoms of all people living in the U.S. Below is a summary of the Bill of Rights:

Amendment 1: All people have the right to **worship** in their own way. They also have freedom of speech. This means they can say anything they want to say. People also have the freedom of the press. They may print anything they want, as long as they believe it to be the truth.

All people have the right to gather peacefully in public meetings. People can write letters to the government saying what they do or do not like.

Amendment 2: People have the right to own weapons.

Amendment 3: In times of peace, Americans cannot be forced to shelter soldiers in their homes.

Amendment 4: Police may not search a person's home without a **warrant**. The warrant must be signed by a judge. It must state exactly what the police are looking for and where they will search.

Amendment 5: In order to charge a person with a crime, the court must follow certain steps. These steps are called **due process of law**. An accused person cannot be forced to be a **witness** against himself or herself. If found innocent of a certain crime, a person cannot be put on trial again for that same crime.

Amendment 6: People arrested for a crime must be told right away why they have been arrested. They have the right to a lawyer. They have the right to a **trial by jury**. They must be present at the trial, and they may have witnesses speak on their behalf.

This young woman, arrested for shoplifting, is being told her rights.

Amendment 7: A person who is suing for a large sum of money in a **civil lawsuit** may have a trial by jury.

Amendment 8: The court may not set bails or fines that are too high. The court cannot set cruel or unusual punishments.

Amendment 9: All rights of the people are protected even if they are not listed in the Constitution.

Amendment 10: Any **power** that has not been given by the Constitution to the federal government belongs to the states or to the people. ■

THINK IT THROUGH

What's in the Bill?

Directions: Read each statement below. If it states a right or freedom guaranteed by the Bill of Rights, write *T* for true. If the statement is not correct according to the Bill of Rights, write *F* for false. The first one is done for you.

__T__ 1. You may read books that other people think should be burned.

_____ 2. You have the right to attend any church that you wish.

_____ 3. If you don't like something that the president has done, you can write a letter to him or her about your beliefs.

_____ 4. You have the right to gather with others in a peaceful protest.

_____ 5. Police can search your house at any time, even if they do not have a search warrant.

_____ 6. The court may not force you to be a witness against yourself.

_____ 7. If you are arrested, police do not have to tell you the reason why.

_____ 8. Though you are found innocent in a criminal case, the court can charge you again for that same crime.

_____ 9. If you are suing someone for a large sum of money, you may have a trial by jury.

_____ 10. If you cannot afford a lawyer, you must defend yourself in court.

ANOTHER LOOK

Think of all the times you have heard TV actors say, "I have rights" or "Read me my rights." They are talking about part of the Bill of Rights.

Imagine that you are arrested for a crime that you did not commit, but there is no Bill of Rights to protect you.

On the lines below, write three rights that you would no longer have. (Refer back to Amendment 6 on page 36.)

1. _____

2. _____

3. _____

VOCABULARY

amendment
a law that is added to the U.S. Constitution

civil lawsuit
a court case involving money or property

constitution
a document that lists the laws and beliefs of a nation or state

due process of law
steps that must be followed when a person is accused of a crime

power
control or authority

trial by jury
a trial in which a group of citizens listens to a court case and decides guilt or innocence

warrant
a legal paper that allows police to search a place or make an arrest

witness
someone who gives evidence at a trial

worship
to honor or revere

VOCABULARY PRACTICE

Part 1: Use Bill of Rights Terms

Directions: Use a word from below to fill in each blank and complete each sentence.

amendment   due process   petition
power   trial by jury   warrant

1. If the police think that someone has drugs in his home, they must get a _____ to search the house.

2. The president of the United States has the _____ to make treaties with other countries.

3. The right of 18-year-olds to vote was granted in an _____ added to the U.S. Constitution in 1971.

4. The Woman's Club sent a _____ to Congress asking that more help be given to daycare.

5. When John was accused of stealing one million dollars, he had a _____.

6. "If the court did not follow _____ _____, maybe my son can go free," Mrs. LaRosa said anxiously.

Part 2: More Than One Meaning

Directions: The words *power* and *witness* can be used in many different situations. Fill in each blank below with the correct word. Remember, their meanings will change slightly depending on the sentence.

power   witness

1. Romeo's new car has _____ brakes.

2. Did you _____ the accident at the corner of Mill and Parker streets?

3. Because she saw the robber's face as he tried to escape, Pam will be a _____ at the trial.

4. Congress has the _____ to reject a president's veto.

WORD ATTACK

Begin It!

- The Williamses **repaid** their loan to the bank.
- Their phone bill is still **unpaid**.

Re- and *un-* are common beginnings, or **prefixes**. In the sentences above, *re-* and *un-* have been added to the main word *paid*.

Now you try it. Start with the main word *cover*, and add the prefixes *re-* and *un-* to it:

re + cover = _____   un + cover = _____

Did you write the words *recover* and *uncover*?

The chart below shows some common words that contain either the prefix *re-* or *un-*. Check to see how many you have seen or used before.

re + *word*	un + *word*
rewind	unable
rebuild	undone
remarry	unclear
remodel	unhappy

PRACTICE

Directions: Read the paragraph below. Each incomplete word is missing either the prefix *re-* or *un-*. Write the correct prefix on the blank lines to complete each word. The first one is done for you.

Laura Jennings is __un__ happy. Her television
              1

set and stereo were stolen last month. The police

have been _____ able to _____ cover them. She
            2   3

must still _____ pay the money that she borrowed
            4

to buy them.

Laura is also nervous. She can't seem to

_____ wind. "I wish I could _____ do everything
   5   6

that has happened," she said.

39

FOR FUN
Using the Library

Suppose you want to find an old issue of *People* magazine or the addresses of some discount stores. Where would you go to find them?

One good place would be your school or public library. Most libraries save past issues of magazines and have phone books for different cities and states. You can also use libraries for every other kind of research. They carry maps, car repair books, child care books, even videotapes.

Call or visit your local library, and find the answers to the questions below.

1. What days and hours is the library open?
   _____

2. Name two newspapers that the library carries.
   a. _____
   b. _____

3. What are two magazines that the library carries?
   a. _____
   b. _____

4. Find the reference section. Name two references that you could use in your studies.
   a. _____
   b. _____

5. What are two subjects you'd like to know more about? When you go to the library, ask for help on how to research these subjects.
   a. _____
   b. _____

Crossing the Border

I am a lucky man. I live in Mexico, but I work in the United States. I have working papers so that I may enter and leave the United States without any trouble. My boss in Idaho got them for me three years ago. Before that, I sneaked across the border in any way that I could.

After being in the U.S. for some time, some workers decide to become U.S. citizens.

Mexico is a very poor country. It is hard to earn enough money to support your family. That is why every year I come to El Norte. (That is what we Mexicans call the United States.) Here, I earn lots of money working the fields.

Someone told me that hundreds of Mexicans cross the border every day. They, too, want to earn money. Many have no working papers, however. They must sneak across. They must always live and work in the shadows. If they are caught by police, they are sent back to Mexico.

I noticed a big difference between my country and the United States. In Mexico, there is a sense that we are one kind of people—Mexicans. That is not so in El Norte. Americans are many kinds of people.

My boss was born in Idaho, but his parents are from the Philippines. His parents came to the United States because they could not make a living in their country. His wife is from Northern Ireland. Her parents sent her to El Norte when she was a young girl. They did not want her to live in a war zone.

I have stopped at many U.S. stores that are owned by Arabs, Chinese, or Koreans. They are all Americans. I began to wonder about the Americans who are white. Maybe they are another nationality, too. I asked, and many said they are German, Italian, or Polish.

This year, I will ask my boss to sponsor me. If I have a full-time job, I can live in El Norte all year round. I will earn enough money to bring my family here. My children will have a better life. They will go to school and learn to be something. Maybe they could become doctors and teachers. Maybe, like my boss, they could someday own a business.

SKILL BUILD

Finding Unstated Main Ideas

As you know, the main idea of a paragraph is often stated in the first or last sentence. Some paragraphs, though, have an **unstated main idea**. If you can't find the main idea in a paragraph, just remember that all the details support one thought. By concluding what that thought is, you can find the main idea.

The paragraph below is from the passage you just read. Read it again, then put a check (✓) beside the correct main idea.

> Someone told me that hundreds of Mexicans cross the border every day. They, too, want to earn money. Many have no working papers, however. They must sneak across. They must always live and work in the shadows. If they are caught by police, they are sent back to Mexico.

_____ **(a)** Many Mexicans work in the United States without working papers.

_____ **(b)** Some Mexican workers want to earn money.

_____ **(c)** Many Mexicans are sent back to Mexico.

You should have put a check beside (a). Now find the main idea of the paragraph below.

> My boss was born in Idaho, but his parents are from the Philippines. His parents came to the United States because they could not make a living in their country. His wife is from Northern Ireland. Her parents sent her to El Norte when she was a young girl. They did not want her to live in a war zone.

_____ **(a)** Northern Ireland is not safe.

_____ **(b)** The United States is a safer place to live.

_____ **(c)** People from other countries come to live in the United States for different reasons.

The answer is (c). The details in the paragraph all tell why some people move to the United States.

▼ POINT TO REMEMBER

To find the main idea when it is not stated directly, ask yourself, "What *one thought* does each detail in the paragraph support?"

UNSTATED MAIN IDEA PRACTICE

Directions: Read each paragraph below, then circle the correct unstated main idea.

1. John's mouth watered as he looked at the restaurants around him. He stared at the picture of tacos in the window before him. He smelled pizza from two doors down. He looked at the Vietnamese restaurant across the street. He had never tried that kind of food before.

   The unstated main idea is:

   (a) John likes to walk.
   (b) John has many kinds of food to choose from.
   (c) John can smell pizza from two doors down.

2. Ms. Williams looked around her U.S. history class. Twelve students were from Vietnam. One girl was from Iran, and another had just arrived from Spain. Three other students were from countries in Central America. Ms. Williams wondered whether many of the students would understand her.

   The unstated main idea is:

   (a) All of the students in Ms. Williams' class speak English.
   (b) Ms. Williams' students are from many different countries.
   (c) Three of Ms. Williams' students are from Central America.

3. The English settled along the Atlantic coast of the New World. At the same time, Spanish towns could be found in Florida and in the Southwest. On the cold Alaskan coast, Russians were building hunting settlements.

   The unstated main idea is:

   (a) People from several countries in Europe settled in the New World at the same time.
   (b) The English found the best area in the New World to settle.
   (c) Europeans all settled near each other in the New World.

ONE MORE STEP

What is one issue that you feel strongly about? For example, you may believe that men and women should have equal pay for the same job or that taxes should be lower.

On the lines below, write a short paragraph about your belief. Write your opinions without stating the main idea directly.

When you finish, ask a friend to find your unstated main idea.

_____
_____
_____
_____
_____
_____
_____
_____
_____
_____
_____
_____
_____
_____
_____

A Nation of Immigrants

Who in your family first came to the United States? Was it you? Your parents? Your great-great-grandparents?

Almost everybody in the United States comes from a family of **immigrants**. Immigrants are people who leave their native country. They go to another country to live.

Some immigrants come to the United States **legally**. This means that they have a **visa** and a **green card**. Others come **illegally**. This means that they don't have the proper papers to be in the United States.

Legally or not, thousands **immigrate** to the United States. Many hear that the United States is a country of **opportunity**. They believe that they will find jobs for themselves and good schools for their children here.

Others immigrate because of **prejudice** at home. This means they have been treated unfairly because of their race, religion, or political views. In recent years, for example, Vietnamese and Cubans have fled war and other **political conflicts** at home. People who flee their country to escape war or other dangers are called **refugees**.

Throughout our nation's history, **waves** of immigrants have come in great numbers. Before 1860, most immigrants were from northern or western European countries such as England, Ireland, and Germany.

Between 1860 and 1920, more than 35 million immigrants came to the United States. Many were from Russia, Italy, Poland, and Austria.

There was less immigration between 1924 and 1948. Congress passed laws to cut down on the number of new immigrants. Between 1948 and 1965, though, laws were made to allow more immigration.

Recently, waves of immigrants have come mostly from Mexico, Asia, the Middle East, Central America, and the Caribbean. When they're qualified, many of these immigrants choose to become U.S. citizens. Watch for news of immigrants on television and in the newspapers. ■

A crowd of immigrants ready to enter the United States at the turn of the century.

THINK IT THROUGH

When and Why?

Directions: Read each question below and circle the correct response.

1. Which wave of immigrants came mostly before 1860?

    (a) English
    (b) Cubans
    (c) Italians

2. Waves of immigrants from Italy, Russia, Poland, and Austria entered the United States between

    (a) 1600 and 1860
    (b) 1860 and 1920
    (c) 1948 and 1965

3. Someone from a poor country would most likely immigrate to the U.S. in order to

    (a) learn a new language
    (b) claim property that someone has given him or her
    (c) make a better life for his or her family

4. Which of the following people is an immigrant?

    (a) Maria, who is visiting from Spain
    (b) Kal, who is an exchange student from Australia
    (c) Gunther, who moved here from West Germany

5. Which of the following immigrants is a refugee?

    (a) someone whose country is divided by civil war
    (b) someone who is running away from his or her parents
    (c) someone who wants to find a better job in the U.S.

6. Which people would most likely belong to a group called the "Korean-American Club?"

    (a) Korean companies that do business in America
    (b) companies in China that do business with each other
    (c) Koreans who now live in the United States

ANOTHER LOOK

Imagine you have decided to move to another country. Where would you go?

_____
_____

What would you have to learn when you got there?

1. _____
_____
_____
_____
_____

2. _____
_____
_____
_____
_____

3. _____
_____
_____
_____
_____

VOCABULARY

green card
a document that allows an immigrant to live in the United States

illegal, illegally
not permitted by law

immigrant
a person who comes to another country to live

immigrate
to move into a foreign country to live

legal, legally
permitted by law

opportunity
a chance to better oneself

political conflict
a fight between two political groups

prejudice
an opinion, often held without good reason, for or against a person, group, or race

refugee
a person who flees his or her country to find freedom or safety

visa
a passport stamp that gives permission to enter a country

wave
a sudden increase in immigration ■

VOCABULARY PRACTICE

Part 1: Work with Immigration Terms

Directions: Complete the sentences. Fill in the blanks with a word from below.

illegal   immigrate   opportunity
refugee   wave

1. Can Le is a war _____ from Vietnam.

2. Eileen Fisher is an _____ immigrant from Ireland because she doesn't have the proper papers.

3. Many poor people from other countries see immigrating to the United States as a golden _____.

4. The first _____ of Irish immigrants came in the late 1600s.

5. The Martinez brothers plan to _____ to Canada next year.

Part 2: More Than One Meaning

Directions: The words *prejudice* and *wave* have more than one meaning. Think about each word, then complete each sentence below.

prejudice   wave

1. Dora has a _____ against jeans and t-shirts.

2. Did you see Roger _____ at Tanya?

3. The tidal _____ killed seven people.

4. Reading about the court case in the paper could _____ the jury members.

5. Lee has a natural _____ to her hair.

WORD ATTACK

Prefix + Word + Suffix

- We are all going to the **event**.
- The Christmas party was **uneventful**.

In the second sentence above, what was added to the word *event*? _____ and _____

You're right if you said that the prefix *un-* and the suffix *-ful* were added to the word *event*. This is a long word, but you can read it easily by breaking it down into these three short parts:

un + event + ful = uneventful

Below are some examples of words that have a prefix, a main word, and a suffix.

re + cover + ing = recovering
un + earth + ly = unearthly
un + lucky + est = unluckiest
un + happy + ness = unhappiness
re + develop + ment = redevelopment

PRACTICE

Directions: Each sentence below contains a word that needs a prefix and a suffix added to it. Use the prefixes and suffixes in the box below to complete each sentence.

Prefix	Suffix
re un	ing ful ly ment

1. The ___un___truth___ful___ boy had few friends.

2. Roy made a _____ adjust _____ to the car's brakes.

3. The town is _____ cover _____ from last week's earthquake.

4. The O'Briens are _____ usual _____ happy today because they are immigrating to Canada next week.

5. Ligaya was _____ friend _____ toward her cousins, who are recent immigrants.

47

FOR FUN

Conduct an Interview

The best way to learn about immigration is to talk with people who have immigrated. They can tell you what it was like to leave their native country and settle someplace new.

Think of someone you know who has immigrated to the United States. Then interview that person to get a sense of what it's like to immigrate.

Before you do your interview, make a list of the questions that you want to ask.

- What country are you from?
- What was your life like there?
- Why did you immigrate to the United States?
- When did you arrive in the United States?
- What did you think of the United States when you got here?

Think of three other questions you would ask, and write them on the blank lines below.

1. _____
2. _____
3. _____

If you do not know an immigrant, interview an older member of your family about life in America when he or she was younger. Questions might include:

- How were things different?
- What was better in the past?
- What do you like better about today?

WORK

Help Wanted

For the week of October 1-7, Entry-Level Job Agency has the following job listings. Applicants must have a high school diploma or GED certificate. Our service is free. All employers will train new workers. If you are hired, we will charge the employer.

SALES AND MARKETING WORK

Customer Service Representative—Airline needs four persons to work 20 hours per week. Must work some evenings and weekends. Duties include helping customers with baggage and flight check-in. Workers must have good communication skills and be able to work under pressure.

Environmental Activist—Nonprofit group seeks part-time and full-time workers. Must be willing to do some travel.

Telemarketers—Need ten full-time workers to sell products over phone. Can work at home or in office. You must have a pleasant voice and strong verbal skills.

SERVICE WORK

Dental Assistant—Children's dental office seeks a warm, cheerful person. Must like to work at a fast pace. Dentist prefers someone who can speak Spanish.

Interpreters—State courts need people who are bilingual in English and one of the following languages: French, Spanish, Tagalog, or Russian. Must be willing to work long hours.

Nanny—Working parents need dependable person to care for two boys, 15 months and 2 years. Light housekeeping also part of duties. You will receive room, board, and salary. Must be a nonsmoker and an English speaker.

Zoo Helper—Children's Zoo needs strong, dependable person to help feed animals and clean cages.

Zoo helpers must work well with people and animals.

PRODUCTION AND TECHNICAL WORK

Baker/Helper—Top dessert company wants someone who can work alone and take pride in doing the best work around. Duties include: cleaning kitchen, preparing pastry dough and frostings, and decorating pastry.

Photo Trainees—Photo lab needs three people to do production work. Job includes working with photo chemicals.

SKILL BUILD

Predicting Words

The sentences below are missing two words. Read both sentences, and try to **predict**, or guess, what the words should be.

> Gary is looking for a new job. So far he _____ applied at two companies. Gary says that one company _____ interested in him.

Now compare your predictions with these below. Notice that there is more than one possible answer to fill the second blank.

> Gary is looking for a new job. So far he **has** applied to two companies. Gary says that one company **is/seems/was** interested in him.

You use predicting skills almost every day. Suppose you missed your bus one morning. You would probably be able to guess what time the next bus would come. You'd be able to predict the time because the buses run on a schedule.

The same is true of language and its patterns. When you listen to a friend and know what he's about to say, you are predicting.

Predicting words can help you read more quickly and with better understanding. It is a skill you probably have already, but you may not yet trust yourself to predict as you read.

To predict words in a sentence, first read the sentence completely. Then choose a word that you think is correct. Read the sentence with the new word to see if it makes sense. If it doesn't, pick another word.

Read the passage below, and try to predict the missing words.

> A law office needs an office helper. Duties include _____(1) phones, filing paperwork, and typing letters. Helper must have _____(2) writing and communication _____(3).

Answers could be: (1) answering (2) strong or good (3) skills.

▼ POINT TO REMEMBER

Predicting words as you read will help you read faster and understand what you read.

PREDICTING WORDS PRACTICE

Directions: Read each paragraph, and predict the missing words. Write your answer on each blank line. Hint: There is more than one correct answer for many of the sentences.

1. My name is Roy Adams. The last five _____, I have
                                         a

   lived in Alaska, but I _____ to California last
                           b

   month. I want to be a waiter, but I can only find work in fast

   food _____. To make money in Alaska, I
          c

   _____ in the fish canneries. I made more
     d

   _____ working there than I make working at a fast
     e

   food place here.

2. My name is Mary Beth Williams. I _____
                                              a

   downtown at Joe's Fast Foods. I hate _____ job. I
                                                 b

   _____ sandwiches and french fries in bags. I only
     c

   stay at this job so that I _____ pay for my
                             d

   schooling. Well, it would also be _____ to meet
                                     e

   that guy from Alaska. I _____ a job where I can
                          f

   work on computers. I'm learning how to work on

   _____ at school.
     g

3. My name is Jerry Garcia. Someday I want to open my own

   restaurant. That's _____ dream. Right now, I
                       a

   _____ two jobs. During the day, I
     b

   _____ the manager at Joe's Fast Foods. At
     c

   _____ I am a chef's helper at a hotel.
     d

ONE MORE STEP

Think of someone you know who is happy with his or her job. Find out why this person likes the job. On another sheet of paper, write a short paragraph about the person and his or her job.

Next, read your paragraph and choose three or four words to leave out. On another sheet of paper, write your paragraph again, but leave those words out. Draw blank lines to show where the words should be. Give your paragraph to a classmate, and ask him or her to predict and fill in the missing words.

51

Career Choices

It's not easy deciding what kind of work to do. For example, what **career** would best suit you if you like to help people? Teaching, politics, social work, and nursing are all careers that can help people. Each one offers entry-level positions.

Most **job counselors** agree that the best way to choose a job or career is to find out more about yourself. Below are some questions about what you like to do. Your answers will help pinpoint the job or career for you.

Asking yourself questions can help you make career choices.

- **Dream jobs**—What kinds of work would you *really* want to do? What would you like about each "dream job"?

- **Interests**—What hobbies and activities do you like? What do you enjoy about each hobby or activity?

- **Talents**—A **talent** is something that comes naturally to you, like dancing, singing, or being friendly. We're always uncovering new talents in ourselves. What would you say are your talents? Which do you really enjoy?

- **Skills**—Most people think that skills are abilities like typing fast or speaking many languages. Actually, a **skill** is anything you can learn or be trained to do well. This includes abilities like talking easily with new people or planning parties.

  Make a list of your skills. You will probably be surprised by how many you have. Then add to your list skills that you would like to learn.

- **Work experiences**—What jobs have you done, paid and unpaid? What jobs have you liked the most and why? Don't overlook work that you have done at home, like cooking and babysitting, or work that you did in school, like fundraising or decorating a gym for a dance. **Volunteer**, or unpaid, work also counts.

- **Values**—Your values should match your career choice. For example, if helping animals is important to you, you might consider being a veterinarian or an animal rights activist.

- **Working conditions**—Here are a few questions to think about. Do you want to work indoors or outdoors? Would you rather work with people, things, or ideas? Do you like to work alone, or do you prefer being around people?

If you're confused by what your answers mean, don't worry. A job counselor will be able to sort through your answers and find patterns. To find a job counselor, look in the phone book under "Career and Vocational Counseling," or call your local community college or state employment office. ■

THINK IT THROUGH

What Do You Do?

Directions: Read each statement and decide which term it describes. Choose the correct word below, and write it on the blank line. The first one is done for you.

> interest   skill   talent   value
> working conditions   work experience

1. Dancing comes naturally to you.
   <u> talent   </u>

2. You work in an old factory that has no windows or fresh air.
   _____

3. You collect rare postage stamps.
   _____

4. In school, you learned to multiply and divide.
   _____

5. Honesty and humor in the people you work with are important to you.
   _____

6. You once taught math at a youth center.
   _____

ANOTHER LOOK

"What are you doing, Mary?" Bruce asked.

"I'm looking for a job, but I'm having a hard time," she said.

"Well, what's your career?"

"Career? Bruce, I said I'm looking for a *job*."

"Mary, get it together. You don't need a job, you need a *career*."

What does Bruce mean? To help you decide, ask yourself this: what is the difference between a *job* and a *career*? Look at the definitions on page 54, or look up both words in a dictionary. Then, on the lines below, write two differences between a job and a career.

1. _____
   _____
   _____
   _____
   _____

2. _____
   _____
   _____
   _____
   _____

53

VOCABULARY

career
an occupation that a person is committed to for a long period of time

experience
skill or knowledge that is learned

interest
a liking or concern for something

job
what a person does to earn money

job counselor
a person who is trained to help you decide on a career and find a job

skill
an ability that is learned, such as reading or writing

talent
a natural ability, such as singing well

volunteer
to do something for free

working conditions
what a workplace is like—busy or quiet, clean or dirty

VOCABULARY PRACTICE

Directions: Read the story below. Then use your predicting skills to fill in the missing words. Use words from below.

> experience   working conditions   skills
> career   interests

Natalie thinks the best _____1_____ for her may be as a firefighter or a probation officer.

One of her _____2_____ is working with people in need. That became clear to her when she looked at her work _____3_____ as a daycare aide.

Natalie has learned many _____4_____ that she could use in either career. But which should she be, a firefighter or probation officer? She can't decide what kind of _____5_____ she likes better, working indoors or outdoors.

WORD ATTACK

Short and Long

When you see the letter *t*, you know that it will sound like the beginning of the word *tap*. Its sound rarely changes because it is a **consonant**. Consonants are simple to read and say because their sounds don't change much.

Vowels, however, can be tricky. Each of the five vowels—*a, e, i, o,* and *u*—has two sounds. Each has a **long sound** and a **short sound**.

Say the letter *a* out loud. Now, say these words: *ate, fate, date, late*. It's easy to hear that the *a* in these words says its own name. This is its long vowel sound.

Below are examples of each vowel's long sound. Practice saying them aloud until they are familiar. The line over the vowels tells you that that vowel has a long sound.

Long Vowel Sounds

ā (ate, fate, date) ō (rope, mope, tone)
ē (deep, meek, team) ū (use, cube, tube)
ī (ice, mine, line)

Now look at the examples below of each vowel's short sound. The dictionary mark ⌣ above a vowel tells you that its sound is short.

Short Vowel Sounds

ă (at, as, pat) ŏ (on, not, mop)
ĕ (end, mend, ten) ŭ (up, cup, luck)
ĭ (it, lip, kit)

PRACTICE

Directions: Say each word below aloud, and decide whether it contains a long or a short vowel sound. Write each word in either the long vowel list or the short vowel list.

| hate | joke | top | cap | send |
| use | mice | key | is | bus |

Long Vowel Words   **Short Vowel Words**

_____   _____
_____   _____
_____   _____
_____   _____
_____   _____

55

FOR FUN

Career and Job Research

Whenever you make a decision, you probably gather all the facts you need and then think carefully about them. Deciding on a job or career is no different.

You can get information about jobs and careers by talking with people about what they do. You can also do research at the library. Books have been written about different careers and jobs. The U.S. Department of Labor has published two helpful books: the *Dictionary of Occupational Titles* and the *Occupational Outlook Handbook*. Both books tell about different jobs and describe the skills, experiences, education, and training you need to do them.

1. What are two jobs or careers that you think you might like?

   a. _____

   b. _____

Find out more about these jobs by talking to friends or reading one of the books named above. Write both jobs at the top of two separate sheets of paper. Then answer questions 2-7 about each job.

2. What duties would you perform on the job?

3. What skills do you need for the job?

4. What kind of education and training do you need for the job?

5. What kind of work experiences would you need to qualify for the job?

6. Do you think there will be a lot of these jobs in the future?

7. Are you still interested in this job? Why or why not?

Waiting

In the lobby of the employment office, job hunters waited to see their job counselors. Sandy Nelson and four others had been waiting for about a half hour.

Sandy looked at Lynn, the young woman sitting across from her. "Is this your first time here?"

"No, this is my third visit," said Lynn. "My counselor is going to do a pretend job interview with me today. She says it will help me feel comfortable in the real ones."

"Really? I didn't know they would do that."

"Oh, yes. The job counselors are very helpful," said Lynn. "A year ago, I came here for a workshop on job hunting. That workshop helped me get my job at a bakery."

"Do you like your job?" asked Sandy.

"Well, yes, but I don't see myself selling cake the rest of my life. Last week, my counselor here helped me decide what careers I might be interested in. Since I don't have any experience working in offices, we put together a resumé that shows my skills and talents."

"I'm glad to hear that," said Sandy. "I'm going back to work after seven years of taking care of my children. I'd rather do something other than bookkeeping. I don't know what my college degree can get me."

"I hope to get a college degree someday," said Lynn. "I've already taken some courses that will help me get a job with a large company. My job counselor tells me that many companies help pay for your studies."

"I've been looking in the want ads," said Sandy. "The jobs I want are either already filled when I call or require more experience. Even though I worked twelve years at bookkeeping jobs, I feel like I'm starting all over again."

"Lynn Calica," announced the receptionist.

Lynn stood up. "Goodbye—and good luck finding a job." ■

A job counselor gives tips on how to start a job hunt.

SKILL BUILD

Infer It

Imagine that you're reading the job advertisements in a newspaper and you see this ad.

> Part-time driver needed to deliver newspapers. Prefer someone with own van or pickup. Must be 18 years or older. See Chuck at Ace Delivery, 644 Morris Street, between 3 and 5 P.M.

To know whether you should apply for a job, you must make **inferences**, or draw conclusions, by carefully reading each fact you are given. Read the ad above one more time, then put a check (✓) in front of the best inference below.

_____ **(a)** This job could turn into full-time work.

_____ **(b)** Chuck was the driver for Ace Delivery before he got a promotion.

_____ **(c)** You will be more likely to get this job if you own your own van or truck.

Did you check (c)? The ad never states that this job could become full-time or that Chuck used to be a driver. The ad *does* state that they "prefer" someone who owns a van or pickup truck.

Now practice making another inference based on the same ad above. Put a check (✓) in front of the best inference.

_____ **(a)** You would start working at 3:00 P.M.

_____ **(b)** If you are 17, you cannot apply for the job.

_____ **(c)** You would deliver newspapers every morning and night.

The best answer is (b). The ad states that you must be at least 18 to apply.

POINT TO REMEMBER

To make an inference, think of all the facts that are given in the reading passage, and ask yourself, "What is the most sensible conclusion?"

INFERENCE PRACTICE

Directions: Read the job advertisements below, then circle the best inference.

1. Well-known auto dealer seeks hard-working salespeople. Experience good, but not required. Great commission/benefits package. Call Miller Wright, 866-4198.

    (a) You could be hired for this job even if you don't have auto sales experience.
    (b) The auto dealer is hiring men only.
    (c) You won't get a salary on this job.

2. Fun Castle now open! We're hiring cashiers, game attendants, and restaurant staff. Part-time and full-time, including nights and weekends. $4.25-$5 per hour, depending on experience. Apply weekdays at 1533 Herne Blvd.

    (a) If you are hired, you will work all three jobs.
    (b) Fun Castle would be willing to hire an experienced worker at $6 per hour.
    (c) If you are hired, you may have to work nights.

3. We need an experienced floral designer for silk and fresh flowers. Will work with weddings and parties. Send resumé to P.O. Box 1032, c/o this newspaper.

    (a) You cannot apply for this job in person.
    (b) You don't need any experience for this job.
    (c) You will make only fresh flower designs for weddings.

4. Counselors needed for nonprofit drug prevention project. Will work with ages 4 to 12. Experience not necessary. Part-time.

    (a) Counselors must be between the ages of 4 and 12.
    (b) This nonprofit group probably counsels children not to use drugs.
    (c) You should have experience working with children.

ONE MORE STEP

Cut out a job advertisement from a newspaper, and read it carefully. Then, on the lines below, write two inferences that you can make from reading the ad. Attach your ad below.

1. _____

2. _____

Starting a Job Hunt

Looking for a job can be a job itself. Applying for jobs listed in the newspaper is a good start, but it's sometimes not enough.

To improve your chances, **apply** to places that aren't advertising for workers. They may not have a job opening right now, but they might in the future.

Here's a plan to help get you started.

1. Decide on a job **objective**. That's a short, clear statement about the type of work or career you want. For example, your objective might be to help children aged five to ten learn arts and crafts.

2. Make two lists. First, write all the **entry-level jobs** that you are interested in. If you want to work with children, you might apply for a job as a teacher's aide or a helper in a children's ward.

    On your second list, write all the places—such as schools, hospitals, and companies—where you would like to work. Write the names, addresses, and phone numbers. Call each one and ask for the name of their **personnel director** and his or her exact title. Make sure you have the right spelling of names and titles.

3. Write a **resumé**. State your job objective near the top. Then list all your skills and experiences—paid and unpaid jobs, education, and training—that relate to your job objective. Your resumé should not be longer than one page. A good-looking resumé does make a difference. If you can't type, pay someone to type it for you.

4. Think of two or three people who can serve as your **references**. A reference is someone who knows you well as a friend or employee. A person who interviews you may phone the references you give to find out more about you.

5. Write a **cover letter** to go with each resumé you send out. Each cover letter should state who you are, why you are interested in the company or organization, and why you are the best **applicant** for the job. At the end, say that you will call to set up a job interview.

6. Now mail your job packet—cover letter and resumé—to each personnel director on your list. Make a follow-up call several days later. Talk with the person who has your resumé, and ask for a job interview. Before you make the call, practice what you want to say. A job counselor or library book on job hunting will help.

   Last, feel **confident**. Be prepared for the no's, but keep in mind that you deserve a job and could do it well. If a job doesn't turn up in six months or so, look at your job-hunt plan. Is it realistic? You may want to go over it with a job counselor. ∎

How should this woman prepare for her interview?

THINK IT THROUGH

Planning the Hunt

Directions: Answer each question below. If you want to, refer back to the passage on page 60.

1. Is it possible to apply for a job at a company that isn't currently advertising?
   _____
   _____

2. What is a job objective?
   _____
   _____

3. What two lists should you make?
   a. _____
   b. _____

4. What should you put in a resumé?
   _____
   _____
   _____

5. What should your cover letter state?
   _____
   _____
   _____

6. Is it a good idea to plan a job hunt? Why or why not?
   _____
   _____
   _____

ANOTHER LOOK

Suppose you sent a resumé and cover letter to a company. You hope to get an interview at the company, and you are now calling the personnel director, Mr. Boyd.

On the lines below, write down what you would say to Mr. Boyd.

MR. BOYD: Hello, this is Mr. Boyd.

YOU: _____
_____

MR. BOYD: Yes, I received your resumé, and I was impressed. However, we don't have a job opening at this time.

YOU: _____
_____
_____
_____

MR. BOYD: Yes, I would like to meet you. How about Tuesday morning at 11 o'clock?

YOU: _____
_____
_____
_____

VOCABULARY

applicant
someone who has applied for a job

apply
to ask in a formal way for a job

confident
sure of yourself

cover letter
a letter that introduces a job applicant; it is usually sent with a resumé

entry-level
jobs for which experience isn't needed

objective
a goal or purpose

personnel director
the person in charge of hiring workers

reference
a person who can give information about a job applicant

resumé
a record of a person's work experience, skills, training, and education

VOCABULARY PRACTICE

Part 1: Use Job Hunt Terms

Directions: Read each sentence and fill in the missing word or words. Use the words that are below.

cover letter   personnel director
reference   job counselor   resumé

1. You can ask a _____ _____ at the state employment office for help.

2. As a _____, you might use a teacher, minister, or counselor who knows you well.

3. The _____ _____ of a large company will know what jobs are open.

4. Make sure you write a job objective on your _____.

5. If you're sending your resumé to anyone, make sure you also have a _____ _____.

Part 2: More Than One Meaning

Directions: You've learned one meaning for the words *apply* and *objective*. Check a dictionary for other meanings. Read the sentences below and fill in the correct word.

apply   objective

1. Maria's job _____ is to be hired as a union carpenter.

2. Jason has decided to _____ himself to his studies so that he can become a top-rate teacher.

3. Mr. Boyd must be _____ when he interviews people for job openings.

4. Will Donald _____ for the job?

5. The new work rule will _____ to all workers.

WORD ATTACK

Break It Up: VC/CV Rule

Try to say these two pretend words aloud: *cav* and *jlmn*.
Which word is easier to say? _____
Which word looks more like a real word? _____

You probably found that the word *cav* is easier to say. It also looks more like a real English word.

Cav is easier to read and say because it contains a vowel *and* consonants. The pretend word *jlmn* contains only consonants. It is impossible to say. Real words *always* contain patterns of both vowels and consonants. These patterns form syllables.

As you know, breaking words into syllables can help you pronounce and read new words correctly. But how do you break a new word into syllables?

Look below at how the word *lesson* is divided into syllables. The vowels and consonants on either side of the break are marked VC and CV. Now you do the same with the other two words.

vc/cv
les/son   whis/per   per/son

Look for the VC/CV Rule when you're breaking new words into smaller parts.

PRACTICE

Directions: Each of the words below can be divided according to the VC/CV rule. On the blank line by each word, write the word again, showing the VC/CV pattern and the correct syllable break.

1. office vc/cv of/fice
2. written _____
3. letter _____
4. forgive _____
5. contact _____
6. collect _____
7. mistake _____
8. practice _____
9. ribbon _____
10. carton _____
11. dinner _____
12. golden _____

FOR FUN

Getting Ready!

Here's a worksheet to help you start your job hunt. This information will come in handy when you write your resumé, complete a job application, or answer questions in a job interview.

1. What is your job objective?
   _____

   Example
   To find a position as a baker's helper

2. List paid work experiences. Write the company's name, your job title, dates of employment, and job duties. (If you need more space, continue on another sheet of paper.)

   Job: _____
   _____
   _____

   Job: _____
   _____
   _____

3. List your education and/or training that qualifies you for this type of job.
   _____
   _____

4. List the skills that qualify you for this type of job.
   _____
   _____

   Example
   Am good at math and reading; can lift 25-pound bags of flour

5. List volunteer work that would qualify you for this type of job.
   _____
   _____

   Example
   Help parents cook meals for church socials

6. List three references. (Choose people who have known you for at least one year. Don't use relatives.) Write their names and job titles, how many years they have known you, and their phone numbers.

   a. _____
   b. _____
   c. _____

Making It Work

Just three years ago, Mary Moses and her four children got by on her income of $4,200 a year. This year, as owner of Mary's Meals, she will make close to $115,000.

What are Mary's ingredients for managing a successful business? "Hard work, a sense of humor, support from my family, and a strong belief in myself," says Mary. Her business is making home-cooked meals and delivering them to people's homes and offices.

Mary learned to cook at age 14 when her mother became sick. "My father, bless his soul, was my only cooking teacher. After mother died, I did all the cooking."

By age 31, Mary had four children to raise. For three years she worked two jobs.

"I was working day and night. I hardly saw the kids. What was worse, most of my pay went to babysitters. Then, when the oldest started to get in trouble, I quit."

Mary applied for public aid and stayed home. For extra money, she and her children made and sold homemade sandwiches and brownies to nearby grocery stores and coffee shops.

One day, the coffee shop owner asked Mary to cook for a party. Within a few months, Mary was cooking for other parties. Mary thought about opening a catering service, but she decided there was too much competition.

Mary's meal delivery service started when Mary had a friend over for dinner. "She ate out maybe five times a week," Mary explains. "I kept teasing her until finally she said, 'Well, Mary, you just send me some home-cooked meals to eat.'"

Many other women are starting businesses on their own, too.

"A few days later I was asking for interviews at every bank in town. I needed a $5,000 loan to start Mary's Meals. People at the banks liked the idea, but they said I was a poor investment. I was a single mother with four children, and I was on welfare."

Mary went to a grocery store owner for advice. He told her how to put together a business plan for the first three years. After Mary got her plan ready, she went back to the banks. One bank finally offered her a loan of $2,000. With a laugh, Mary says, "I made $10,000 that first year!" ∎

SKILL BUILD

More on Inferring

People who give loans or hire workers make a lot of inferences. They make conclusions about a person's character and work habits. They observe how a person behaves in an interview, and they look closely at how a job or loan application is completed.

For example, a personnel director might notice that Lester Smith, a job applicant, answered every question on his job application carefully and completely. The director might then **infer** an important fact—Lester Smith can finish a job that's given him.

Just like personnel directors, we make inferences every day. We often use inference skills when we read. Read the paragraph below. What one inference can you make from the details? Put a check (✓) in front of each statement that is a reasonable inference.

When Joanna got to the office, she was sweaty and covered with dirt. Her car had a flat tire on the way there. She glanced at her watch—2:45. Forcing a smile on her face, Joanna said to the secretary, "Good afternoon. I am Joanna Williams, and I have a 2:30 job interview."

_____ **(a)** Joanna fixed the flat tire herself.

_____ **(b)** Joanna was late for her first day on the job.

_____ **(c)** Joanna was not happy that her watch was broken.

Sentence (a) is the correct inference.

Clues: Joanna is sweaty and covered with dirt.

These clues tell you that Joanna fixed the flat tire herself.

▼
POINT TO REMEMBER

An inference is a logical conclusion that is not stated directly. When you read a passage, read all the details carefully. They are clues that can lead to good inferences.

INFERENCE PRACTICE

Directions: Read the passages below. What one inference can you make from the details that are given? Circle the best inference. Then write the clues that led you to your inference.

1. Every day for six months, Rudy has run five miles and worked out in the weight room. In two weeks, he will take the fitness test again. He knows he can pass it on his second try. "Next March," he thinks, "I'll be one of the city's firefighters."

   (a) Rudy was a weakling before he started exercising.
   (b) Rudy didn't pass the fitness test on his first try.
   (c) Rudy used to be a firefighter.

   Clues: _____
   _____
   _____

2. Sal watched his classmates march onto the football field. He could have been marching right behind Charlie. Sal had only needed to finish two classes. Instead, he got a job washing dishes. "Who am I fooling?" Sal thought. "I wish I were getting my diploma too."

   (a) Sal has received his diploma already.
   (b) Sal was late for graduation because he was working.
   (c) Sal had dropped out of school.

   Clues: _____
   _____
   _____

3. "Why do you think you are qualified to be my assistant manager?" asked Ms. Yu, the restaurant owner. "Well," said Amy, "I worked in my uncle's restaurant during high school. I waited on tables, cleared them, and set them. I washed dishes and helped prepare some of the food. I also counted the money at the end of the day."

   (a) Ms. Yu works for Amy's uncle.
   (b) Amy is applying for a job at Mrs. Yu's restaurant.
   (c) Amy's uncle is looking for an assistant manager.

   Clues: _____
   _____
   _____

ONE MORE STEP

What is your best quality? (For example: friendly, hardworking, good cook)

My best quality is

_____
_____
_____

Below, write two facts that show this is your best quality. Make sure that anyone reading these facts would be able to infer your best quality.

Fact: _____
_____
_____
_____
_____

Fact: _____
_____
_____
_____
_____
_____

The Job Interview

You've just been called for a job interview. It's next week. You should be happy, but instead you're nervous.

You can calm your nerves by preparing yourself. That's right, do homework for a **job interview**. First, learn all you can about the type of job you are applying for. You can go to the public library and find a **job description** in the *Dictionary of Occupational Titles*. You can also talk to someone who has experience with the same kind of job.

Second, learn something about the company or organization: what it produces, how much it makes a year, how many employees it has. Your public library or **chamber of commerce** should have information about companies in your area.

Not many people realize they can ask questions during a job interview. In fact, asking questions often **impresses** an **interviewer**. So, your third piece of homework is to make a list of questions. Think of facts that you'd like to know about the company. You might ask, "How has your company grown in the last three years?" or "What opportunities for **promotions** does this job offer?"

Once you have gathered information about the job and the company and made a list of questions, practice your interview skills. You can ask a friend or a job counselor to **role-play** with you. Make up a list of questions that interviewers often ask, and give the list to a friend. Dress for the pretend interview just as you would for the real one, and practice answering each question.

The day of your job interview, think positively. Give yourself plenty of time to get there. You can even arrive early if it would make you feel more confident. If you must bring a friend, leave him or her outside the door.

When you meet the interviewer, shake his or her hand. Repeat his or her name aloud so that you remember it. Let the interviewer take the lead in the conversation. Don't feel rushed to answer any question. Remember, you don't have to answer questions that are **unrelated** to whether you could do the job well. For example, you don't have to tell an interviewer whether you are married, or whether you want to have children someday. Just ask politely how the question relates to the job.

When the interview is over, shake the interviewer's hand. Thank him or her for the interview. When you get home, write a thank-you note and send it to the interviewer. This important last step can mean the difference between getting or not getting a job. ■

Why does preparing ahead of time help an interview go well?

THINK IT THROUGH

You Be the Job Counselor

Directions: The sentences below describe each step in Carl Hopkins's job hunt. Read each sentence and decide whether what Carl did helped or hurt his employment chances. Then put a check in the correct column. The first one is done for you.

	Helped	**Hurt**
1. Carl read the job description of a library aide in the *Dictionary of Occupational Titles*.	✓	
2. Carl thought of a list of questions to ask during an interview.		
3. Carl and his job counselor role-played an interview.		
4. Carl brought his best friend with him to meet Ms. Reynolds.		
5. Carl arrived ten minutes late for his interview with Ms. Reynolds.		
6. After Ms. Reynolds introduced herself, Carl shook her hand.		
7. Carl asked Ms. Reynolds, "What can a library aide be promoted to?"		
8. Carl didn't send Ms. Reynolds a thank-you note for the interview.		

ANOTHER LOOK

Jean Benson just had an interview at Smith Electronics. During the interview, she held her one-year-old son on her lap. When the interviewer asked her what job she wanted, Jean said, "Oh, it doesn't matter. Whatever you think is best." Do you think Jean will be hired? Why or why not?

VOCABULARY

chamber of commerce
a group that works to help businesses in their community grow

Dictionary of Occupational Titles
a reference book that describes many different jobs

impress
to make someone think of you well

interviewer
a person who asks someone questions in order to learn more about that person

job description
a written statement that tells about a job

job interview
a meeting between an employer and a job applicant

promotion
a raise to a higher position

role-play
to act a part

unrelated
not connected, having no relation ■

VOCABULARY PRACTICE

Part 1: Work with Interview Terms

Directions: Read each sentence below carefully, and decide which word (or words) in parentheses completes the sentence correctly. Circle the correct answer. The first one is done for you.

1. The (*job description*/*job interview*) states that one of your duties would be washing all lab tools.

2. He is Marc Johnson, the (*chamber of commerce/interviewer*) from Home Computer, Inc.

3. The job counselor will (*role-play/impress*) an interview with you.

4. "I like to see (*confidence/role-play*) in a person," said the interviewer.

5. Mae's (*confidence/job interview*) is at 2:30 P.M. on Monday.

6. Tony learned all about a welder's job from the (Dictionary of Occupational Titles/*promotion*).

Part 2: More Than One Meaning

Directions: The words *promotion* and *impress* both have different meanings. Fill in each blank below with the correct word.

promotion   impress

1. "Did you get the _____ to supervisor?" asked Judy.

2. Matt hopes he can _____ his boss as being a hard worker.

3. Taylor Toys is giving away samples of their new products as a _____.

4. The postal clerk must _____ a postmark before putting the package in the mail.

5. Many parents try to _____ upon their children that honesty is important.

WORD ATTACK

Break It Up: V/CV Rule

Say the word *solo* aloud. How would you divide this word into syllables? _____
You're right if you divided the word like this: so/lo (v cv)

The word *solo* follows the V/CV Rule (vowel/consonant + vowel). Each word below also follows this pattern:

      v cv   v cv   v cv   v cv
     re/turn mo/tel pre/pare rea/son

Now say these words aloud and listen to the first vowel sound in each (the *e* in *return*, the *o* in *motel*). Can you tell what these vowel sounds all have in common? _____

If you said they are all long vowels, you're right. Remember, long vowels can be shown like this: rēturn, mōtel.

If a first syllable has a long vowel sound, divide the word between the vowel and the next consonant: V/CV.

PRACTICE

Part 1: Use One Rule

Directions: Read the words below aloud. They all follow the V/CV pattern. On each blank line, write the word and show where it should be divided.

1. nation nā/tion
2. repeat _____
3. local _____
4. evil _____
5. libel _____
6. promote _____
7. beware _____
8. deceive _____

Part 2: Use Two Rules

Directions: Decide whether each word below should be broken down according to the VC/CV Rule or the V/CV Rule. On the blank lines, show how each should be divided. Two are done for you.

1. coffee cŏf/fee
2. belief bē/lief
3. blossom _____
4. service _____
5. open _____
6. detail _____
7. arrive _____
8. pretend _____

71

FOR FUN

Getting It Right!

When you set up a job interview, it's very important to get names, dates, and numbers right. Always make sure you take down the following information correctly:

- name of business
- name of interviewer, his or her job title, and phone number
- address where you'll be interviewed
- day and time of interview

Last week, Walter sent his resumé to David's Clothing Store. He has just gotten a phone call from Mr. Bonner. Read their conversation, then answer the questions below.

MR. BONNER: Hello, may I speak with Walter Chung?

WALTER: Yes, this is Walter.

MR. BONNER: This is John Bonner, the personnel director at David's Clothing Store. You sent us your resumé, and I'm wondering if you're still interested in a sales position.

WALTER: Yes, I'm interested, Mr. Bonner.

MR. BONNER: Can you come in Thursday morning, say at 11?

WALTER: That's fine. Should I come to the store?

MR. BONNER: No, I work at the main office on 251 Page Street.

WALTER: 251 Page Street. Is there a room or suite number?

MR. BONNER: Yes. We're on the second floor, room 218. If you need to contact me, my phone number is 866-9750.

WALTER: 866-9750. Mr. Bonner, is your name spelled B-O-N-N-E-R?

MR. BONNER: Yes, that's right. I'll see you Thursday, Walter.

WALTER: Thank you again. Good-bye, Mr. Bonner.

1. What is the name of the business? _____
2. Who is the interviewer? _____
3. What is his job title? _____
4. What is his phone number? _____
5. Where will the interview take place? _____
6. When is the interview? _____

SCIENCE

Are You What You Eat?

Many parents use myths, or old sayings, to get their children to eat. Nutritionists study food myths. They have found that many of these old sayings, such as "Fish is brain food," contain some truth. Eating fish may not make people smarter, but it *can* help prevent heart disease.

Let's check some other food myths.

Myth: Eating carrots gives you good eyesight.
Fact: Carrots are high in vitamin A, a nutrient that helps us see in bright and dim light.

Myth: An apple a day keeps the doctor away.
Fact: Apples are rich in potassium, a nutrient that our bodies need. Apples are also a good source of pectin and fiber. Pectin slows down the body's absorption of fat, and fiber helps clean the digestive tract. Before you eat apples or other fruits, though, wash them well. This will clean off any harmful chemicals, or pesticides, that have been sprayed on them.

Myth: Eating carbohydrates, such as breads, potatoes, and rice, will make you fat.
Fact: The body needs carbohydrates the same way a car needs gasoline. Whether or not you gain weight from carbohydrates depends on the kind that you eat. Natural carbohydrates, found in fruits, vegetables, grains, and nuts, have few calories and many nutrients. Refined carbohydrates, found in cakes, candies, and cookies, have many calories but few nutrients.

Myth: You are what you eat.
Based on what you know now, do you think there's any truth to this saying? ■

If you watch the news or read the newspaper, you probably have heard reports about the foods we eat. You may have heard that oat bran can help prevent cancer or that certain pesticides used on fruit can cause cancer. To avoid any possible dangers, eat small amounts of many kinds of foods. The foods to the left are just some of those available to consumers.

SKILL BUILD

Compare and Contrast

Suppose you're in the fresh-fruit section of a grocery store. How would you decide which fruits to buy? Most likely, you would **compare** the fruits, or see how they are alike. You would also **contrast** the fruits, or see how they are different.

Comparing and contrasting are important reading skills. They are also important life skills. They can help you get the most for your money, decide which job to take, or choose which car to buy.

Sometimes a chart can help you see the similarities and differences between two things. Read the following passage, then fill in the facts to complete the chart below.

> Finally, Al narrowed his choice down to either white or whole-wheat bread. He read each label. The whole-wheat bread had 24 servings for $1.89. But, at only $1.15 for 24 servings, the white bread seemed to be a better deal.
>
> "Dad," said his son, "get the white bread. It only has 70 calories per slice. This whole-wheat has 80."
>
> Al remembered all the ads on TV about eating right. Then he put the whole-wheat bread in the cart.

	White	**Whole-Wheat**
1. cost	a.	b.
2. number of servings	a.	b.
3. calories per serving	a.	b.

In what ways are the breads alike? How are they different? Check your answers: **1. a.** $1.15, **b.** $1.89; **2. a.** 24, **b.** 24; **3. a.** 70, **b.** 80.

Both breads have the *same* number of servings. The breads are *different* in cost and calories per serving.

▼
POINT TO REMEMBER

Comparison is seeing how two or more things are alike; contrasting is seeing how they are different.

COMPARE AND CONTRAST PRACTICE

Directions: Read the two grocery ads below. Compare and contrast the two stores by filling in the chart.

Bell Supermarket

OPEN 24 HOURS

PRODUCE
Celery . . . . $.79 ea.
Apples . . . . $.49 lb.

FROZEN VEGETABLES
Corn (8 oz.) . . . . 3 for $1
Spinach (8 oz.) . . . . $.60 ea.

DAIRY PRODUCTS
Yogurt . . . . 2 for $.59
Jumbo Eggs . . . . $.89 dozen
Cheddar Cheese . . . . $1.69 lb.

Sale Prices Good: August 23–August 26

Fulton Market

SALE!!!
August 20–August 30

FRUITS/VEGETABLES
Carrots . . . . 1.09 3 lb.
Fresh Pineapples . . . . 2.04 each

DAIRY
Gallon Milk 1.60
Cheddar Cheese . . . . 1.89 lb.

MEAT/POULTRY/FISH
T-Bone Steak . . . . 3.40 lb.
Whitefish . . . . 2.56 lb.
Turkey . . . . 1.09 lb.

6 A.M. – 11 P.M. Daily

	Bell Supermarket	**Fulton Market**
1. What are the store hours?		
2. When does the sale begin and end?		
3. What kinds of fish are on sale, if any?		
4. What kinds of vegetables?		
5. What kinds of dairy goods?		

ONE MORE STEP

Suppose you work evenings. You get off at 10 P.M. and usually shop for food then.

At which of the two stores would you choose to shop, Bell Supermarket or Fulton Market? _____

Why would you pick that store? _____

Where do you go to do your shopping? _____

Why do you go to that store? _____

75

The Four Food Groups

Nutritionists, or food scientists, tell us we should eat a **variety** of foods. That way, our bodies will get all the **nutrients** necessary for good health. How can we get the right nutrients? What do nutritionists mean by a variety of foods?

To help people understand good nutrition, nutritionists divide food into **food groups**. Each group gives us certain nutrients, like **protein** or vitamin A. Many nutritionists divide food into these four basic groups:

- fruits and vegetables
- grain products (bread, cereal, pasta)—whole grain and **enriched**
- meats and nonmeat **alternatives**
- milk products

The chart below lists the four food groups and shows what major nutrients each group provides. It also suggests the **minimum**, or fewest, number of servings from each group that a child, teen, adult, and pregnant woman should eat each day. Notice that different foods have different serving sizes.

Food Group	Major Nutrients Provided	Suggested Minimum Daily Servings
Fruits/Vegetables Serving size: ½ cup	**carbohydrates, vitamin** A, vitamin C	FOUR SERVINGS: child, teen, adult, and pregnant woman
Grain Products Serving size: ½ cup	carbohydrates, thiamine, riboflavin, niacin	FOUR SERVINGS: child, teen, adult, and pregnant woman
Meats and Nonmeat Alternatives Serving size: 2-3 oz.	protein, iron, thiamine, niacin	TWO SERVINGS: child, teen, and adult THREE SERVINGS: pregnant woman
Milk Products Serving size: 8 oz. liquid or yogurt, 1 oz. cheese	vitamin D, calcium, protein, riboflavin	THREE SERVINGS: child FOUR SERVINGS: teen and pregnant woman TWO SERVINGS: adult

THINK IT THROUGH

Serve It Up

Part 1

Directions: Match each term on the left with the correct set of examples on the right. The first one is done for you.

__e__ 1. nutrients

____ 2. four food groups

____ 3. meats/nonmeat alternatives

____ 4. fruits and vegetables

____ 5. milk products

____ 6. grains

(a) enriched white bread, rice, corn tortillas, muffins

(b) yogurt, cheese, nonfat dry milk, ice cream

(c) milk, meat/nonmeat alternatives, fruits and vegetables, grain products

(d) corn, okra, apples, peas, oranges

(e) proteins, fats, vitamins, minerals

(f) peanut butter, beans, chicken

Part 2

Directions: How many daily servings should each person below have from each food group? Look back at the chart on page 76 for help.

1. Loy, age 5:
   ____ a. fruit and vegetable
   ____ b. grain
   ____ c. meat/protein
   ____ d. milk

2. Teresa, pregnant, age 32:
   ____ a. fruit and vegetable
   ____ b. grain
   ____ c. meat/protein
   ____ d. milk

3. Al, age 14:
   ____ a. fruit and vegetable
   ____ b. grain
   ____ c. meat/protein
   ____ d. milk

4. Lester, age 52:
   ____ a. fruit and vegetable
   ____ b. grain
   ____ c. meat/protein
   ____ d. milk

ANOTHER LOOK

Plan three meals for yourself for one day. Use the chart on page 76 to make sure you're getting the minimum daily servings for each food group.

Breakfast: _____

Lunch: _____

Dinner: _____

VOCABULARY

alternative
a choice, or option

carbohydrate
a nutrient that gives the body immediate energy

enrich
to improve the nutritional value of food by adding one or more vitamins or minerals

food groups
the four basic types of food needed every day for good nutrition

minimum
the smallest amount

nutrient
a part of food: carbohydrate, protein, fat, vitamin, or mineral

nutritionist
a person who studies the nutritional value in food

protein
a nutrient that makes the body grow and stay strong

variety
a sampling; many different kinds

vitamin
any nutrient that the body needs for good health ■

VOCABULARY PRACTICE

Part 1: Work with Nutrition Terms

Directions: Complete each sentence with the correct word from below.

alternative   minimum   nutrition
enriched   nutrient   variety

1. You can buy orange juice that has been _____ with calcium and vitamin D.

2. Some people prefer to eat one or two types of food rather than a _____ of different foods.

3. If you want to lose weight, following guidelines for healthy _____ makes more sense than a fad diet.

4. Ed's mother makes sure he drinks a _____ of eight glasses of liquid each day.

5. Combining corn, beans, and a milk product is an _____ nonmeat source of protein.

6. Vitamin A is one _____ in broccoli.

Part 2: More Than One Meaning

Directions: Check a dictionary for different meanings of the words *enrich* and *variety*. Then fill in the blanks below.

enrich   variety

1. May likes to _____ her homemade bread by adding bran.

2. Tom never realized the _____ of vegetables he could eat.

3. This year's graduating class put together a _____ show.

4. Music and art _____ many people's lives.

5. The Kims enjoy a _____ of sports.

WORD ATTACK

Break It Up: VC/V Rule

Take a look again at how the word *solo* is divided into syllables: so/lo.

As you know, the word *solo* follows the V/CV Rule: so/lo. It is divided after the first long vowel sound.

Now say the word *solid* aloud. Listen carefully to the *o* sound. How is it different from the *o* in *solo*? _____

You're right if you said that the *o* in *solid* is a short vowel. Short vowels sound like the vowels in these words: *cap, ten, bin, top, cup*.

How would you divide the word *solid* into two syllables? _____ The correct way to break this word down is: sol/id.

This syllable break follows a new pattern. It is called the VC/V rule. Whenever the first vowel in a word is a *short* vowel, use the V/CV rule. If you get confused, think back to these key words:

sō/lo (V/CV)   sŏl/id (VC/V)

PRACTICE

Part 1: Use One Rule

Directions: Each of the words below follows the VC/V rule. Use this rule to break each word into syllables. Then label the VC/V pattern. The first one is done for you.

1. menu mĕn/u
2. divide _____
3. balance _____
4. level _____
5. salad _____
6. value _____
7. product _____
8. liver _____

Part 2: Use Two Rules

Directions: Read the three words below aloud. *Two* of them follow the V/CV rule, and the other follows the VC/V rule. Listen carefully to the first vowel sound in each, then divide each word into syllables.

1. digest _____
2. fiber _____
3. stomach _____

FOR FUN

Be a Label Reader

Food products sold in the United States must have food labels that tell what is in them. The labels on this page show the kinds of information you will find on every package.

FRONT OF PACKAGE

Name of product

Net weight
This tells how much the product weighs, or how much is inside it. The weight is often given in both standard (ounces) and metric (grams) units.

BACK OF PACKAGE

Servings per container: 24
Serving size: 1 rice cake
calories.....................20
fat...................0.23 grams
protein...............0.44 grams
sodium.............16 milligrams
carbohydrates.........4.42 grams
fiber..................0.18 grams
Contains less than 2% of the U.S. RDA of protein, Vitamin A, Vitamin C, thiamine, riboflavin, niacin, calcium, and iron.

Nutritional Information (per serving)
This tells you how many calories and nutrients are in each serving.

Ingredients: brown rice, sesame seed, rice syrup, salt

Ingredients
A list of everything, from largest to smallest amount, that goes into making the product

Eastern Rice Products, Inc.
2481 Ala Wai Street, Keeomuku, HI

Name and address of the company that makes the product

PRACTICE

1. What is the name of this product? _____

2. How much does it weigh or contain? _____

3. What ingredient does the product have the smallest amount of?
   _____

4. How much of the following does one serving of the product contain?

   (a) calories _____

   (b) fat _____

   (c) protein _____

   (d) carbohydrates _____

5. Suppose you were not satisfied with this product. Where would you write to complain? _____

The Battle Against AIDS

On Peter and Mandy Linnel's TV set is a picture of their daughter, Barbara. The picture shows a laughing, healthy child on her second birthday.

These pictures were taken almost one year ago. The thin, cranky child in her mother's arms doesn't look at all like the baby in the picture. Barbara now has AIDS.

Children under 13 with this deadly disease are not unusual. Between 1983 and 1987, the Centers for Disease Control counted 563 cases of children with AIDS. Experts believe that during those five years, another 2,000 children were infected with the virus that usually leads to AIDS. They think that by 1991 the number of AIDS-infected children will be between 10,000 and 20,000.

How do children catch AIDS? Most are infected before they are born, while still in their mother's womb. Dr. Maria Ferrer, an AIDS researcher, states, "Many people don't realize that an unborn child can catch a virus. If a woman who has the AIDS virus becomes pregnant, the chances are very high that her baby will contract the virus. AIDS may not show up when her baby is born, but the baby will always be in danger of developing the disease."

In Barbara's case, AIDS did not appear for almost two years. Just after Barbara's second birthday, she caught a cold. When she was not well a month later, the Linnels began to worry. They took her to a doctor, but he could find nothing wrong.

"Peter came home with a *Newsweek* article about children with AIDS," said Mandy. "We read it and got very scared. Peter and I each dated many people before

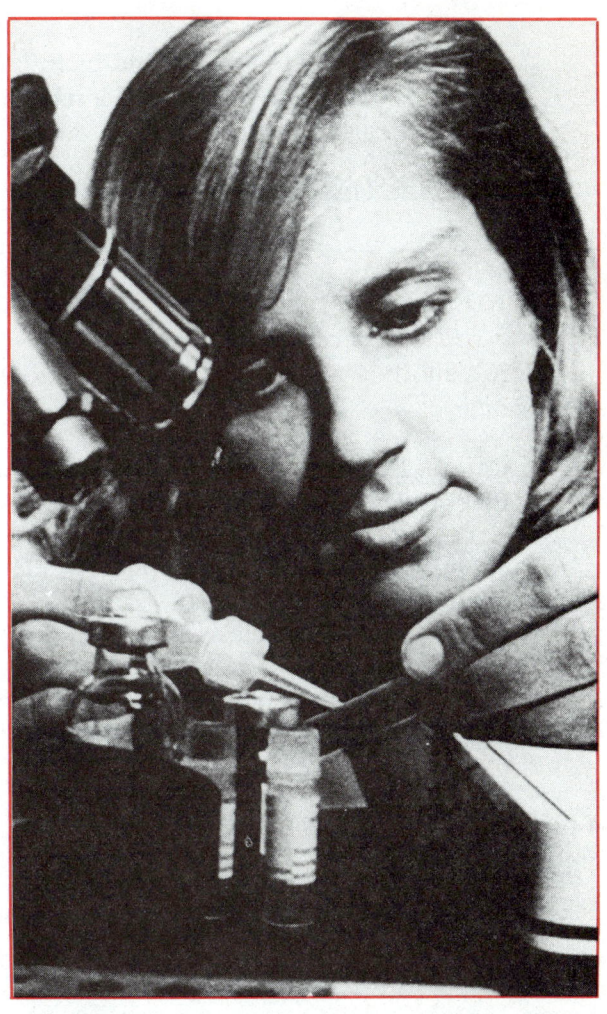

One weapon in the fight against AIDS is medical research.

we were married. We realized that one of them could have infected us."

The Linnels both took an AIDS-antibody test, and both tested positive. When they had Barbara tested, her results were also positive. Doctors then diagnosed Barbara as having AIDS.

Mandy decided to quit her job and stay home with Barbara. "Barbara is a very brave child," Mandy said. "I hope she knows that we love her, and that we are very sorry for what we have given her." ■

SKILL BUILD

Cause and Effect

Just after Barbara's second birthday, she caught a cold. When she was not well a month later, the Linnels began to worry.

Why did the Linnels start to worry? _____

_____

Your answer is probably something like this: *Their daughter Barbara still had a cold after one month.*

Here's another way to sum up the relationship between these two events:

Cause: Barbara still had a cold after one month.
Effect: The Linnels began to worry.

A **cause** makes something happen. An **effect** is a result, or what happens because of a cause.

Now read the quote below. It is from the reading on page 81.

"Peter came home with a *Newsweek* article about children with AIDS. . . . We read it and got very scared."

Which statement below better states the cause described in the sentence above?

_____ **(a)** Peter brought home an article about children and AIDS.

_____ **(b)** Peter guessed why Barbara was sick.

If you said that statement (a) is the cause, you're right.

Now, which statement below better states the *effect* described in the sentence?

_____ **(a)** Peter and Mandy got a divorce.

_____ **(b)** Peter and Mandy became frightened.

The correct answer is statement (b).

▼ POINT TO REMEMBER

To find a cause-and-effect relationship, ask these two questions:
"What made something happen?" (the cause)
"What happened?" (the effect)

CAUSE AND EFFECT PRACTICE

Directions: Read each passage below. Then read the cause or the effect that is already given. In your own words, fill in the missing information (either the cause or the effect).

1. Colds, flus, smallpox, and herpes are all caused by viruses. A virus is a very small parasite that enters the body. When it infects certain cells, a person gets sick.

   Cause: A flu virus infects a person's body.

   Effect: _____

2. Soon after a virus infects a person, his immune system goes to work. The immune system begins to produce antibodies. The antibodies work to kill the virus, and the person gets well.

   Cause: _____

   Effect: A person gets well.

3. The first cases of AIDS were reported in 1981. At first, people paid little attention to the disease. But as thousands of men, women, and children became infected and died, more money was put into AIDS research.

   Cause: _____

   Effect: More money was put into research on AIDS.

4. In 1986, Cleve Jones's best friend died of AIDS. In his friend's memory, Jones sewed a panel for a quilt. Today, this quilt has several thousand panels and is known as the AIDS Quilt. Each panel has been sewn for someone who died of AIDS.

   Cause: Cleve Jones sewed one quilt panel for a friend who died of AIDS.

   Effect: _____

ONE MORE STEP

Think of a scene that you remember well from a movie or TV show. On the lines below, tell what happened in that scene. Then state the cause and effect of the scene.

What happened? _____

Cause: _____

Effect: _____

83

The Facts About AIDS

As of 1988, over 82,000 Americans had died from the disease called **AIDS**. At that time, more than one million Americans had the **virus** that often leads to AIDS.

AIDS, or Acquired Immune Deficiency Syndrome, destroys the body's **immune system**. The virus that often leads to AIDS is known as **HIV**.

Some researchers still believe that it's possible to be **infected** with HIV without developing AIDS. Once people are infected, though, they will carry HIV the rest of their lives. They will always be capable of infecting others.

HIV is drawn to **white blood cells**, which protect the body from disease. When HIV becomes active, it takes over the white blood cells and **multiplies**. AIDS develops when HIV has spread throughout the body and has destroyed the immune system. The body then becomes infected with viruses and cancers that lead to death.

Although AIDS is a **contagious**, or catchable, disease, it is hard to **transmit** between persons. The virus *cannot* be transmitted, or passed on, through casual contact. It can't be **contracted** by shaking hands with, hugging, or kissing an HIV-infected person. It can't be contracted by sharing food or drinks or by breathing the same air. Researchers also know that HIV can't be transmitted by insects such as fleas or mosquitos.

HIV can only be transmitted through blood-to-blood contact or semen-to-blood contact. So far, most AIDS patients and HIV-infected persons have contracted it through sexual contact or sharing drug needles.

Everyone is at risk of contracting HIV—men, women, children, even unborn babies. But, armed with the facts, people can stop AIDS from being transmitted. ■

Marching together is one way to lend support and lessen fear of AIDS.

THINK IT THROUGH

Just the Facts

Directions: Complete each sentence below by circling the correct response.

1. AIDS, or Acquired Immune Deficiency Syndrome, is

    (a) an illness that goes away after a few weeks of rest
    (b) a disease that severely damages the immune system
    (c) a virus

2. AIDS is thought to be caused by

    (a) white blood cells called HIV
    (b) a cancer called HIV
    (c) a virus called HIV

3. The immune system is important because it

    (a) circulates blood in the body
    (b) passes nutrients to every cell in the body
    (c) fights off infection and disease

4. People can catch AIDS if

    (a) they are bitten by an HIV-infected mosquito
    (b) the blood from an HIV-infected person enters their bloodstream
    (c) they drink from the same glass as an HIV-infected person

5. If a person is infected with HIV, he or she

    (a) can infect other people
    (b) will definitely die from AIDS
    (c) can get a cure for it

ANOTHER LOOK

Some people are so afraid of catching AIDS that they refuse to sit in the same room with an AIDS patient. The only way to cure this fear is through education. If people know what AIDS is, how it can be "caught," and how it can be prevented, their fears will lessen.

How can people learn about AIDS? Think of three ways to educate people in your community, then write your ideas on the lines below.

1. _____
   _____
   _____
   _____
   _____

2. _____
   _____
   _____
   _____
   _____

3. _____
   _____
   _____
   _____
   _____
   _____

VOCABULARY

AIDS
a disease that destroys the body's immune system

contagious
able to be spread from person to person

contract
to catch a virus or disease

HIV (Human Immunodeficiency Virus)
the virus that often leads to AIDS

immune system
the system that fights off infection and disease

infect, infected
to make diseased

multiply, multiplies
to increase

transmit
to pass on a sickness to another person

virus
a very small organism that can cause disease

white blood cells
cells that fight off infection and disease ■

VOCABULARY PRACTICE

Part 1: Work with AIDS Terms

Directions: Read the story below. Then fill in the missing blanks with the correct words from below.

contagious   infect
virus   contract   transmit

Cold weather is often the time that the flu _____ hits. It's a very _____ disease. Small children can _____ the flu
                     1   2   3
virus to each other very easily.

How do children _____ each other
                              4

with the flu virus? Suppose that a child with the flu sneezes into her hand and puts her hand on a desk. Another child puts his hand on the same spot. He

will most likely _____ the virus within a
                          5

few days.

Part 2: More Than One Meaning

Directions: You've learned one meaning for the words *contract* and *transmit*. Look up other meanings for each word in a dictionary. Then complete the sentences below by writing the correct word on the blank.

contract   transmit

1. The school district will _____ the cheapest roofer to repair the damages.

2. You can hear things while you're swimming under water because water will _____ the sounds.

3. Daisy Lewis signed a _____ for a $1,000 loan.

4. A wool sweater will shrink, or _____, if it's washed in hot water.

5. "I hope I don't _____ color blindness to my children," said Tony.

WORD ATTACK

Break It Up: VC/CV, V/CV, and VC/V Rules

For a review of the three syllable rules you've learned, look at the chart below. Remember, the mark – over a vowel tells you it's a long vowel. The mark ⌣ over a vowel tells you it is a short vowel sound.

VC/CV Rule	V/CV Rule	VC/V Rule
bet/ter	vī/rus	sĕc/ond
col/lege	fē/tus	dĭv/ide
num/ber	bē/low	mĭn/ute

PRACTICE

Directions: Decide which pattern each word below follows. First divide the words into syllables, using the correct rule. Then write the rule on the right. The first one is done for you.

1. disease   _dis/ease_   _VC/V Rule_
2. pregnant
3. result
4. table
5. major
6. bigger
7. medal
8. final
9. native
10. never

FOR FUN

What's the Hypothesis?

When scientists began to study AIDS, they probably started with a hypothesis like, "AIDS is caused by a virus." A **hypothesis** is a possible explanation for something. After making a hypothesis, scientists work to prove it true or false.

Scientists make many hypotheses about health and the environment. What ideas have you wondered about in those areas? Read the hypotheses below. On the blank lines, describe how you would prove each hypothesis true or false.

HEALTH

Hypothesis: Noise pollution can cause hearing loss.
How could you prove or disprove this hypothesis?

I would test the hearing of a group of people before they were around loud noise. After they were around noise pollution, I'd test their hearing again.

Hypothesis: Regular exercise can lower blood pressure.
How could you prove or disprove this hypothesis?

_____
_____
_____

ENVIRONMENT

Hypothesis: Car pollution can kill green plants.
How could you prove or disprove this hypothesis?

_____
_____
_____

"No Smoking!"

If you smoke, you may resent others telling you not to. If you don't smoke, you may become upset by cigarette smoke. Sometimes these conflicts can only be decided in a court of law.

Q: Mr. Martin, tell us in your own words what happened at 1:15 P.M. on September 18.

A: I went into Joe's Cafe to get some lunch. After ordering, I lit a cigarette. About five minutes later, Mr. Valdes told me to stop smoking. I told him to mind his own business.

Q: What did Mr. Valdes say then?

A: He said, "Your cigarette *is* my business. The smoke is making me sick." When I refused to stop smoking, he threw his water at me.

Q: What did you do then?

A: I hit him with my briefcase.

Q: Mr. Martin, was there a "No Smoking" sign near where you were sitting?

A: No, there wasn't.

LAWYER: Thank you, Mr. Martin.

(Mr. Valdes takes the stand.)

Q: Mr. Valdes, did Mr. Martin ever face you directly as he smoked his cigarette?

A: Well, no, but . . .

Q: So, Mr. Martin could not have blown smoke into your face?

A: No. But I know when there's a cigarette close by. The stench makes me sick.

Q: Mr. Valdes, are you aware that you were sitting in a smoking section?

A: That's a lie! The place didn't have a "No Smoking" section. I looked when I came in. Every restaurant should have a "No Smoking" section so people like that can't . . .

LAWYER: Thank you, Mr. Valdes. No further questions. ■

Smoking in public places often causes conflict between people.

SKILL BUILD

Sequencing

In the passage you just read, Mr. Martin describes the events that took place between himself and Mr. Valdes. Of course, he tells those events in **sequence**, or in the order that they happened. If he didn't, you'd never understand what went on!

Like finding a main idea or comparing and contrasting, sequencing is another important reading skill. To make sure you understand and remember what happens in a passage, try to picture events in your mind as you read them. Picturing Mr. Martin holding a cigarette or Mr. Valdes with an angry expression can help you remember which man does what in the story.

Read Mr. Martin's testimony again, and try to visualize each step that he describes.

Read the events below, then number them in the correct order. The first one is done for you.

_____ Mr. Valdes tells Mr. Martin to stop smoking.

_____ Mr. Martin sits at a table close to Mr. Valdes.

__1__ Mr. Martin enters Joe's Cafe.

_____ Mr. Martin hits Mr. Valdes with his briefcase.

_____ Mr. Valdes throws water on Mr. Martin.

You should have listed your answers in this order: 3, 2, 1, 5, 4.
 Now put the events below in the correct order.

"Where is that shopping center?" moaned Linda. She pulled into a gas station and asked for directions.
 First, the attendant drew a map for her. Then he said, "Go two blocks on Hunter, then take a right on Post. Drive five blocks, and you'll be there!"

_____ The gas station attendant drew a map for Linda.

_____ Linda pulled into a gas station.

_____ Linda lost her way to the shopping center.

_____ The attendant told Linda the way to the shopping center.

Now check your answers. The correct order is: 3, 2, 1, 4.

▼ **POINT TO REMEMBER**

Picturing what is happening can help you understand what you read. It can also help you remember the correct sequence of events.

SEQUENCE PRACTICE

Directions: Read each passage below, then read the statements that follow. You'll see that the statements are presented in the wrong order. Put the events in the correct order by numbering them.

1. Mae Lee has worked for 12 years at the same company. When she first started, she could smoke at her desk. Last year, the company made a new policy. Workers could smoke only in the third-floor lounge. Mae worked on the seventh floor, so she often sneaked a smoke at her desk. Her supervisor warned Mae twice not to do this. When he caught her the third time, he fired her. She is now suing the company to get her job back.

____ Mae is fired.

_1_ The company makes a new policy that workers can smoke only in the third-floor lounge.

____ Mae sues for her job back.

____ Mae is warned not to smoke at her desk.

2. Super Airlines used to get complaints about the smoking sections on their planes. Two years ago, they banned smoking on flights of 40 minutes or less. Airline executives believed they would gain more customers than they would lose with this policy. One year later, Super banned smoking on all flights of two hours or less. Last month, executives announced they were banning smoking on all flights.

____ Smoking is banned on flights of 40 minutes or less.

____ The airline allows smoking on all flights.

____ Super bans smoking on flights of two hours or less.

____ The airline bans smoking on all flights.

3. Ten minutes after running for the bus, Mr. Kim was still gasping for air. He thought he would faint. Mr. Kim started to read his newspaper, and this headline caught his eye: *47 Million Americans Addicted to Cigarettes*. Mr. Kim wondered if he was addicted since he smokes half a pack every day.

____ Mr. Kim wonders if he is addicted to smoking.

____ Mr. Kim reads his newspaper.

____ Mr. Kim feels faint.

____ Mr. Kim runs to the bus.

ONE MORE STEP

How to make toast. How to pump gas. How to diaper a baby. Each of these tasks has a certain series of steps. Think of something that you do every day. What sequence of steps do you follow?

Task: _____

_____

_____

_____

Steps:

1. _____

_____

_____

_____

2. _____

_____

_____

_____

3. _____

_____

_____

_____

Smoking and the Respiratory System

Every day, more "No Smoking" signs go up in restaurants, banks, and other public places. In fact, many public health officials have a goal. This goal is to have no more smokers by the year 2000. Can this goal be reached? Will Americans heed the warning that smoking can kill?

Research shows that smokers have a higher risk of **developing** cancer of the mouth, larynx, and lung. All of these are part of the body's **respiratory system**.

The respiratory system's job is to take in **oxygen** and remove **carbon dioxide** from the body. You complete one **cycle** each time you breathe in and out. Here's how it works.

You breathe in air through your nose or mouth. The air passes through your windpipe, or trachea. The trachea leads to hundreds of tubes, which become smaller as they lead into tiny air sacs in your lungs. Oxygen enters the **bloodstream** through the air sacs. The bloodstream then carries the oxygen to every part of your body.

The bloodstream also carries carbon dioxide from all parts of your body to the air sacs. There, the **waste** goes up through the tubes to the windpipe and out of your mouth or nose as you breathe out.

Each time a person breathes in smoke from tobacco products, he also breathes in **tar** and other chemicals. A build-up of these waste products can lead to illness and disease. For example, when chemicals build up in the air sacs, the sacs have a harder time taking in oxygen and removing carbon dioxide. Eventually, the lung cells become damaged or cancerous. ■

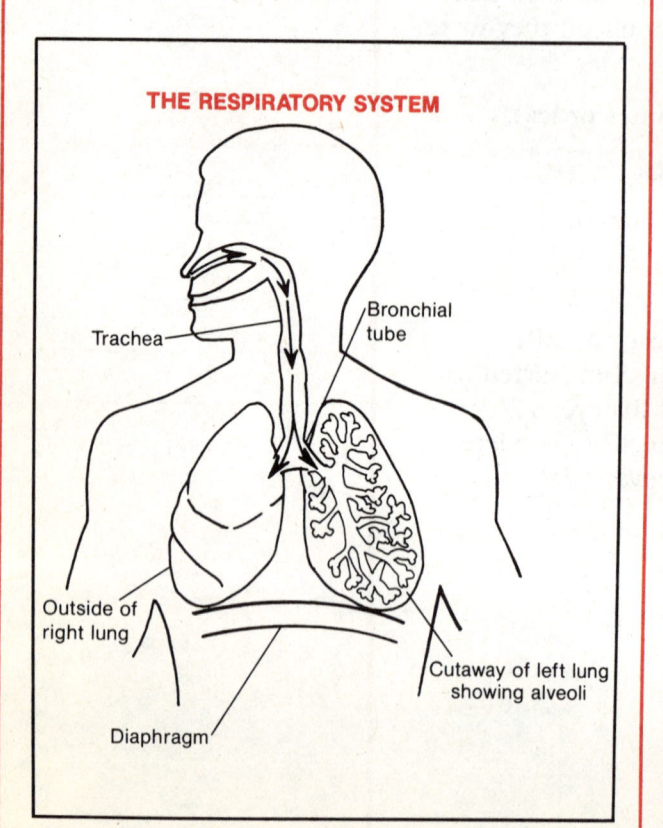

THE RESPIRATORY SYSTEM

- Trachea
- Bronchial tube
- Outside of right lung
- Cutaway of left lung showing alveoli
- Diaphragm

THE PASSIVE SMOKER

Nonsmokers used to be **victims**. They coughed and felt sick from the smell of cigarette smoke in homes, workplaces, restaurants, airlines, and other public places.

Times are changing, though. Strict smoking laws are being passed to protect the nonsmoker.

Why the change? Scientific evidence began showing that nonsmokers are in fact smoking **passively**. This means that their health is affected by the smoky air that they breathe. Studies show that nonsmokers who live or work with smokers have a higher risk of developing smoke-related diseases than those who do not.

THINK IT THROUGH

Full of Smoke

Directions: Circle the correct response to each question below.

1. Smokers have a higher risk of developing

    (a) breast cancer
    (b) lung cancer
    (c) cancer of the pancreas

2. Which system passes oxygen and carbon dioxide in and out of the body?

    (a) digestive system
    (b) nervous system
    (c) respiratory system

3. In order to live, the body needs to take in

    (a) carbon dioxide
    (b) nitrogen
    (c) oxygen

4. Through what part of the body does oxygen pass to enter the bloodstream?

    (a) the lungs
    (b) the trachea
    (c) the heart

5. How does cigarette smoke harm a person's lungs?

    (a) Tar and other chemicals can block the air sacs so that oxygen can't enter the bloodstream.
    (b) The smoke blocks any air from being breathed in.
    (c) The hot smoke burns the lungs.

6. What path do air and smoke follow through the body?

    (a) bloodstream, lungs, trachea
    (b) lungs, bloodstream, trachea
    (c) trachea, lungs, bloodstream

ANOTHER LOOK

More employers are setting strict smoking policies. Some companies forbid their workers to smoke on *or* off the job. Suppose you were a smoker at a company that had that rule. Would you complain that your constitutional rights were being taken away? Why or why not?

_____
_____
_____
_____
_____
_____
_____
_____
_____
_____
_____
_____
_____

VOCABULARY

bloodstream
the course of blood through the body

carbon dioxide
a gas that the body releases when a person breathes out

cycle
a series of steps that repeat themselves

develop
to come about little by little

oxygen
a gas that the body needs and gets when a person breathes in

passive
not active; allowing something to happen

respiratory system
the system that moves oxygen and other gases through the body

tar
solid waste that results from the burning of tobacco

victim
someone who is hurt

waste
gas, liquid, or solid matter that the body makes from oxygen and food ■

VOCABULARY PRACTICE

Part 1: Review the Respiratory System

Directions: Read each sentence below carefully, and decide which word or words make sense. Circle the correct word.

1. Cigarette smoke contains (*oxygen/tar*).

2. Oxygen and carbon dioxide pass through your (*cycle/lungs*).

3. The mouth, larynx, and lungs are all part of the (*respiratory system/bloodstream*).

4. (*Carbon dioxide/Oxygen*) is a gas that the body must get rid of.

5. Research shows that smokers can (*develop/passive*) cancer.

6. Some nonsmokers have been (*victims/waste*) of lung cancer.

Part 2: More Than One Meaning

Directions: You've learned one meaning for each of the words below. They all have other meanings. Read the sentences below, then use a word from below to complete them.

cycle   waste
tar   develop   victims

1. Mr. Randall needed hot _____ to fix the roof.

2. Did the twins _____ or walk to school today?

3. Many elderly persons have been _____ of thieves.

4. Beatrice knew it was a _____ of the company's time whenever she walked to the lounge to smoke.

5. DeMello Photos can _____ color slides for a lower price than the other photo lab.

WORD ATTACK

Syllabication Rules Review

1. **Compound Words** (page 15)
   Divide a compound word between the two smaller words it contains: homework = home/work.

2. **Main Word + Suffix** (page 23)
   Divide between the main word and the suffix (*-ing*, *-er*, *-est*, *-ly*, *-ful*, *-less*): rushing = rush/ing, teacher = teach/er.

3. **Prefix + Main Word** (page 39)
   Divide between the prefix (*re-*, *un-*) and the main word: relearn = re/learn.

4. **Prefix + Main Word + Suffix** (page 47)
   Divide in three places—between the prefix, the main word, and the suffix: returning = re/turn/ing.

5. **VC/CV Rule** (page 63)
   Divide between the two consonants: current = cur/rent.

6. **V/CV Rule** (page 71)
   Divide after the long vowel sound: future = fu/ture.

7. **VC/V Rule** (page 79)
   Divide the word after the short vowel and the consonant: rigor = rig/or.

PRACTICE

Directions: On the line on the left, divide each word in **dark type** into smaller parts. On the right, write which rule you used.

1. Some people say smoking is a bad **habit**.
   _____ _____

2. What kind of **illness** does Mr. Allen have?
   _____ _____

3. The course that blood follows through the body is called the **bloodstream**.
   _____ _____

4. What is the **current** number-one song?
   _____ _____

95

FOR FUN

Keeping a Journal

June 25

Time to celebrate! I scored high on all my tests, and I finally lost ten pounds. Bill, my counselor, is telling me to take a break. I guess I will, but in September I'll sign up for classes. If everything goes well, I should be able to graduate soon.

Mom says I could quit my job and live with her. Then I could go to school full-time. That's nice of her, and last year I would have done it. But I like to do things on my own now.

Many people keep a journal—a written record—about themselves. Some write in their journal every day. Others write once or twice a week.

Writing in a journal gives you more than a record of feelings, people, and events. Journal keeping can improve your reading and writing skills. It can also sharpen your observation and memory skills.

To start, all you need is something to write in. You can use an artist's sketchbook, a wire-bound notebook, or scratch paper stapled together.

Choose a quiet time to write in your journal. You might want to write at that same time each day. Record each date before you start each writing.

As you write, don't worry about spelling, grammar, or punctuation. You can practice those skills later. For now, just get your ideas down on paper.

What should you write in your journal? Anything that you feel like putting down. It might be gossip, a conversation between two people, a copy of a recipe, or just the events of the day. Some journal keepers use their journals to help them sort out their feelings and problems. Read the suggestions below, then write three more.

- the plot of a TV show, movie, or video
- description of someone you know or have met
- _____
- _____
- _____

Answer Key

The Invitation

Five Ws Practice
page 3
1. a. Martha and Ed Baker
   b. baby shower
   c. Sunday, May 10, 4-6 P.M.
   d. 218 Lake Street
   e. Martha and Ed Baker are expecting a baby.
2. a. Kathy Allen and Charles Ferguson
   b. wedding reception
   c. Saturday, September 21, 1-5 P.M.
   d. Golden Gate Park
   e. The couple are getting married.
3. a. Marlene and Al Navarro
   b. anniversary dinner
   c. June 15, 1987, 12 P.M.
   d. Fort Ord Officers Club
   e. It is the Navarros' 50th wedding anniversary.

One More Step
page 3
Answers will vary. Check your responses with a teacher or friend.

What Kind of Family?
page 5
1. nuclear
2. extended
3. nuclear
4. extended
5. extended
6. Answers will vary.
7. Answers will vary.

Another Look
page 5
Answers will vary. Check your responses with a teacher or friend.

Vocabulary Practice
page 6
Part 1
1. (b) parents, children
2. (d) factories, shops
3. (a) Americans, Europeans, Asians
4. (e) parents, children, relatives
5. (c) car, boat, plane

Part 2
1. (b) The structure of an essay is the way its ideas are organized on paper.
2. (c) The structure of a bridge is the way it is built, or constructed.
3. (a) The structure of a plant is the way its smaller parts are put together to form a living thing.

It's a Syllable Practice
page 7

One Syllable	Two Syllables	Three Syllables
love	par/ent	ex/tend/ed
mom	Car/men	nu/cle/ar
home	un/cle	rel/a/tive

A Family Tree
page 8
Answers will vary. Check your response with a teacher or friend.

Single-Parent Dad

Details Practice
page 11
1. a. The new daycare center is for children ages one to five.
   b. The owner's name is Mabel Woods.
   c. The center opened Monday, September 6.
   d. The center is located at 15 River Street.
   e. Daycare is important because many families have two parents who work outside the home.
2. a. Dr. Susan Kubota and Dr. Gene Wong are named.
   b. A parenting class is being offered.
   c. The course will begin in the fall.
   d. It will be taught at City College.
   e. The class will be helpful because no one is born with parenting skills—everyone must learn them.
3. a. Youth Group, Inc., took the survey.
   b. They talked to children about alcohol abuse.
   c. The survey took place last May.

d. Youth Group, Inc., traveled across the country.
  e. The group was concerned about child and teenage alcoholics.

One More Step
page 11
Answers will vary. Check your responses with a teacher or friend.

A Parent's Life
page 13
1. (c) parents
2. (a) parenting
3. (b) Autocratic parents set strict rules for children to follow.
4. (c) Permissive parents let children make their own decisions.

Another Look
page 13
Answers will vary. Check your responses with a teacher or friend.

Vocabulary Practice
page 14
Part 1
1. (c) autocratic
2. (b) permissive
3. (a) authoritative

Part 2
1. style
2. value
3. value
4. style
5. value

Compound Words Practice
page 15
grandfather, grandparent, granddaughter, stepfather, stepparent, stepdaughter, babysitter

Sentences will vary. Have your teacher or a friend check them.

Keeping Dates Straight
page 16
Cheri can go to the baseball game on June 21.

Married or Single?

Restating Practice
page 19
Part 1
1. (c)
2. (a)
3. (d)
4. (b)

Part 2
Sentences will vary. Have your teacher or a friend check your restatements.

One More Step
page 19
Answers will vary. Check your response with a teacher or friend.

Graph It!
page 21
1. F
2. F
3. F
4. T
5. T
6. F
7. T
8. T
9. F

Another Look
page 21
Answers will vary. Check your responses with a teacher or friend.

Vocabulary Practice
page 22
Part 1
1. rate
2. researcher
3. decrease
4. increase
5. curve

Part 2
1. trend
2. rate
3. rate
4. trend

End It Practice
page 23
1. looking
2. standing
3. youngest
4. younger
5. wisely

Crossword Puzzle
page 24
Down
1. love
3. wedding

Across
2. vows
4. children
5. single

Does One Vote Make a Difference?

Summarizing Practice
page 27
1. Answers will vary, but should be similar to: Ben Gonzales has a long record of supporting business.
2. Answers will vary, but should be similar to: Molly Heller cares about family issues.

One More Step
page 27
Answers will vary. Check your response with a teacher or friend.

Signing Up
page 29
1. You must be at least 18 years old in order to vote.
2. You can get an affidavit at the Registrar of Voters or Board of Elections office in your county, or at a voter registration table in a public place like a post office, fire station, police station, or mall.
3. You will know you are registered to vote when you receive your voter registration card.
4. Todd must fill out a new affidavit.
5. No, Layla is not qualified to register since she is only 17 years old.

Another Look
page 29
If people had to pay a tax in order to vote, poor people who could not afford the tax would be most affected. The tax was probably outlawed because people found it unfair and unconstitutional.

Vocabulary Practice
page 30

Part 1	Part 2
1. polling place	1. register
2. citizen	2. register
3. affidavit	3. issue
4. election	4. issue
5. qualification	5. issue
6. register	6. register

More Endings Practice
page 31

Part 1	Part 2
1. yourself	1. hopelessness
2. darkness	2. smilingly
3. masterful	3. faithfully
4. countless	4. forgetfulness

Fill It Out
page 32
Answers will vary.

My Right to Read

Main Idea Practice
page 35
The main ideas in each paragraph are listed below.

1. Our country's first constitution was called the Articles of Confederation.
2. For these reasons, many Americans were unhappy with the Articles of Confederation.
3. In May 1787, twelve of the thirteen states sent representatives to a convention in Philadelphia, PA.
4. These three parts make up the structure of the U.S. Constitution—the preamble, articles, and amendments.

One More Step
page 35
Answers will vary.

What's in the Bill?
page 37
1. T   4. T   7. F   10. F
2. T   5. F   8. F
3. T   6. T   9. T

Another Look
page 37
Answers will vary. Check your responses with a teacher or friend.

Vocabulary Practice
page 38
Part 1
1. warrant   4. petition
2. power   5. trial by jury
3. amendment   6. due process

Part 2

1. power
2. witness
3. witness
4. power

**Begin It Practice
page 39**

1. unhappy
2. unable
3. recover
4. repay
5. unwind
6. undo

**Using the Library
page 40**

Answers will vary. Check your responses with a teacher or friend.

Crossing the Border

**Unstated Main Idea Practice
page 43**

1. (b) John has many kinds of food to choose from.
2. (b) Ms. Williams' students are from many different countries.
3. (a) People from several countries in Europe settled in the New World at the same time.

**One More Step
page 43**

Answers will vary. Check your responses with a teacher or friend.

**When and Why?
page 45**

1. (a)
2. (b)
3. (c)
4. (c)
5. (a)
6. (c)

**Another Look
page 45**

Answers will vary. Check your response with a teacher or friend.

**Vocabulary Practice
page 46**

Part 1
1. refugee
2. illegal
3. opportunity
4. wave
5. immigrate

Part 2

1. prejudice
2. wave
3. wave
4. prejudice
5. wave

**Prefix + Word + Suffix Practice
page 47**

1. untruthful
2. readjustment
3. recovering
4. unusually
5. unfriendly

**Conduct an Interview
page 48**

Questions will vary, but could include "What do you like most about the U.S.?" "How did you travel to the U.S?" or "What is the hardest adjustment you've had to make?"

Help Wanted

**Predicting Words Practice
page 51**

1. a. years/months
   b. moved/came
   c. restaurants/places
   d. worked
   e. money/cash
2. a. work
   b. my/this
   c. stuff/put/pack
   d. can
   e. great/nice (or other acceptable answers)
   f. want
   g. computers/them
3. a. my
   b. have/work/hold
   c. am
   d. night

**One More Step
page 51**

Answers will vary. Check your response with a teacher or friend.

**What Do You Do?
page 53**

1. talent
2. working conditions
3. interest
4. skill
5. value
6. work experience

Another Look
page 53
Answers will vary, but might be similar to: A person can switch jobs many times, but a career is a commitment that lasts a long time.

Vocabulary Practice
page 54
1. career
2. interests
3. experience
4. skills
5. working conditions

Short and Long Practice
page 55

Long Vowel Words	Short Vowel Words
hate	top
joke	cap
use	send
mice	is
key	bus

Career and Job Research
page 56
Answers will vary. Check your responses with a teacher or friend.

Waiting

Inference Practice
page 59
1. (a)
2. (c)
3. (a)
4. (b)

One More Step
page 59
Answers will vary. Check your responses with a teacher or friend.

Planning the Hunt
page 61
1. Yes. You can send your resumé to any company you want at any time. They may agree to interview you right away, or they may keep you in mind for future jobs.
2. A job objective is a short, clear statement that tells specifically what your current job or career goal is.
3. a. a list of entry-level jobs you are interested in
   b. a list of places that hire people to do jobs like these
4. A resumé is a one-page summary of your job objective, past work experience, education, and skills.
5. In your cover letter, you should state your name, why you are interested in that job and company, and why you could do the job well.
6. Yes, you should always plan your job hunt. Otherwise, it's easy to let time go by without doing anything. Also, if you have set realistic goals, you'll be able to figure out if you're not doing something right.

Another Look
page 61
Answers will vary. Check your responses with a teacher or friend.

Vocabulary Practice
page 62

Part 1
1. job counselor
2. reference
3. personnel director
4. resumé
5. cover letter

Part 2
1. objective
2. apply
3. objective
4. apply
5. apply

Break It Up Practice
page 63

VC CV
1. of/fice

VC CV
2. writ/ten

VC CV
3. let/ter

VC CV
4. for/give

VC CV
5. con/tact

VC CV
6. col/lect

VC CV
7. mis/take

VC CV
8. prac/tice

VC CV
9. rib/bon

VC CV
10. car/ton

VC CV
11. din/ner

VC CV
12. gol/den

Getting Ready!
page 64
Answers will vary. Check your response with a teacher or friend.

101

Making It Work

Inference Practice
page 67
1. (b)
2. (c)
3. (b)

One More Step
page 67
Answers will vary. Check your responses with a teacher or friend.

You Be the Job Counselor
page 69
1. helped
2. helped
3. helped
4. hurt
5. hurt
6. helped
7. helped
8. hurt

Another Look
page 69
Answers will vary. Check your responses with a teacher or friend.

Vocabulary Practice
page 70
Part 1
1. job description
2. interviewer
3. role-play
4. confidence
5. job interview
6. *Dictionary of Occupational Titles*

Part 2
1. promotion
2. impress
3. promotion
4. impress
5. impress

Break It Up Practice
page 71
Part 1
1. na/tion — v̄/cv
2. re/peat — v̄/cv
3. lo/cal — v̄/cv
4. e/vil — v̄/cv
5. li/bel — v̄/cv
6. pro/mote — v̄/cv
7. be/ware — v̄/cv
8. de/ceive — v̄/cv

Part 2
1. cof/fee — vc/cv
2. be/lief — v̄/cv
3. blos/som — vc/cv
4. ser/vice — vc/cv
5. o/pen — v̄/cv
6. de/tail — v̄/cv
7. ar/rive — vc/cv
8. pre/tend — v̄/cv

Getting It Right!
page 72
1. David's Clothing Store
2. Mr. Bonner
3. personnel director
4. 866-9750
5. 251 Page Street, room 218
6. Thursday at 11 A.M.

Are You What You Eat?

Compare and Contrast Practice
page 75

	Bell Supermarket	Fulton Market
1.	24 hours	6 A.M.–11 P.M.
2.	Aug. 23–Aug. 26	Aug. 20–Aug. 30
3.	----	whitefish
4.	celery, corn, spinach	carrots
5.	yogurt, eggs, cheese	milk, cheese

One More Step
page 75
Answers will vary. Check your response with a teacher or friend.

Serve It Up
page 77
Part 1
1. (e)
2. (c)
3. (f)
4. (d)
5. (b)
6. (a)

Part 2
1. a. 4
   b. 4
   c. 2
   d. 3
2. a. 4
   b. 4
   c. 3
   d. 4
3. a. 4
   b. 4
   c. 2
   d. 4
4. a. 4
   b. 4
   c. 2
   d. 2

Another Look
page 77
Answers will vary. Check your responses with a teacher or friend.

Vocabulary Practice
page 78
Part 1
1. enriched
2. variety
3. nutrition
4. minimum
5. alternative
6. nutrient

Part 2
1. enrich
2. variety
3. variety
4. enrich
5. variety

Break It Up Practice
page 79
Part 1
1. men/u — vc/v
2. div/ide — vc/v
3. bal/ance — vc/v
4. lev/el — vc/v
5. sal/ad — vc/v
6. val/ue — vc/v
7. prod/uct — vc/v
8. liv/er — vc/v

Part 2
1. di/gest — v/cv
2. fi/ber — v/cv
3. stom/ach — vc/v

Be a Label Reader
page 80
1. Tasty Brown Rice Cakes
2. 5¾ oz. (163 grams)
3. salt
4. a. 20 calories   c. 0.44 grams
   b. 0.23 grams   d. 4.42 grams
5. Eastern Rice Products, Inc.
   2481 Ala Wai Street, Keeomuku, HI

The Battle Against AIDS

Cause and Effect Practice
page 83
Answers will vary.

1. **Effect:** That person becomes sick with the flu.
2. **Cause:** The immune system produces antibodies that attack the virus.
3. **Cause:** Thousands of people became infected with and died from AIDS.
4. **Effect:** The AIDS Quilt, which now has thousands of panels, began.

One More Step
page 83
Answers will vary. Check your responses with a teacher or friend.

Just the Facts
page 85
1. (b)   4. (b)
2. (c)   5. (a)
3. (c)

Another Look
page 85
Answers will vary. Possible answers could include having a town meeting, posting fact sheets in public places, or going from door to door telling people the facts about AIDS.

Vocabulary Practice
page 86
Part 1
1. virus
2. contagious
3. transmit
4. infect
5. contract

Part 2
1. contract
2. transmit
3. contract
4. contract
5. transmit

Break It Up Practice
page 87
1. dis/ease   VC/V Rule
2. preg/nant   VC/CV Rule
3. re/sult   V/CV Rule
4. ta/ble   V/CV Rule
5. ma/jor   V/CV Rule
6. big/ger   VC/CV Rule
7. med/al   VC/V Rule
8. fi/nal   V/CV Rule
9. na/tive   V/CV Rule
10. nev/er   VC/V Rule

What's the Hypothesis?
page 88
Answers will vary. Check your responses with a teacher or friend.

"No Smoking!"

Sequence Practice
page 91
1. The statements should be numbered in this sequence: 3, 1, 4, 2
2. The statements should be numbered in this sequence: 2, 1, 3, 4
3. The statements should be numbered in this sequence: 4, 3, 2, 1

One More Step
page 91
Answers will vary. Check your responses with a teacher or friend.

Full of Smoke
page 93
1. (b) 4. (a)
2. (c) 5. (a)
3. (c) 6. (c)

Another Look
page 93
Answers will vary. Check your responses with a teacher or friend.

Vocabulary Practice
page 94

Part 1
1. tar
2. lungs
3. respiratory system
4. carbon dioxide
5. develop
6. victims

Part 2
1. tar
2. cycle
3. victims
4. waste
5. develop

Syllabication Rules Practice
page 95
1. hab/it — VC/V Rule
2. ill/ness — Main word + Suffix
3. blood/stream — Compound Word
4. cur/rent — VC/CV Rule

Keeping a Journal
page 96
Answers will vary. Possible answers could include (a) what you did with friends last weekend, (b) lyrics to a song or poem, or (c) goals for the future.